Walki
Irel

C000198631

| DISCARDED |

3303463542

DISCARDED

Christopher Somerville

Walking in Ireland

50 WALKS THROUGH THE HEART AND SOUL OF IRELAND

EBURY
PRESS

1 3 5 7 9 10 8 6 4 2

Published in 2019 by Ebury Press, an imprint of Ebury Publishing,
20 Vauxhall Bridge Road,
London SW1V 2SA

Ebury Press is part of the Penguin Random House group of companies whose
addresses can be found at global.penguinrandomhouse.com

Penguin
Random House
UK

Text Copyright © Christopher Somerville 2010
Illustrations © Claire Littlejohn 2010
Cover Illustration © Claire Littlejohn 2010

Christopher Somerville has asserted his right to be identified as the author of this
Work in accordance with the Copyright, Designs and Patents Act 1988

This edition published by Ebury Press in 2019

Design: Bob Vickers
Illustrator: Claire Littlejohn

www.penguin.co.uk

A CIP catalogue record for this book is available from the British Library

ISBN 9781529104820

Typeset in India by Integra Software Services
Prin... ...bound in Great Britain by Clays Ltd, ...S.p.A.

...Penguin... ...mmitted to a ...stainable
...els, our readers and our ...anet.
The book ...orest Stewardship... ...ouncil®

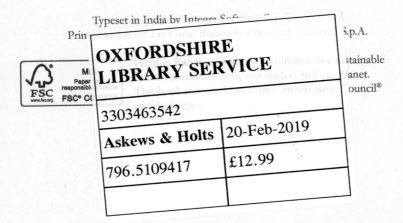

OXFORDSHIRE
LIBRARY SERVICE

3303463542	
Askews & Holts	20-Feb-2019
796.5109417	£12.99

CONTENTS

INTRODUCTION

THIS BOOK IS A selection of 50 of the finest excursions from the Walk of the Week which I contribute to the Travel Section of the *Irish Independent* newspaper. Each walk features one of Claire Littlejohn's beautiful hand-painted picture maps. You'll find history, wildlife, culture, poems, songs, landscape, topography, environmental matters and a whole lot of other wonders. Instructions and practicalities are all taken care of – so all you have to do is grab the book, get your boots on, go out and explore to your heart's content. Here are walks for all abilities, from buggy-friendly forest parks such as Donadea in County Kildare to Diamond Hill in Connemara National Park (a proper mountain that children can proudly top out on) and from long-distance hikes to gentle country strolls. You can access many by public transport; details are included.

The walks range from very well-known landscapes such as Killarney National Park and the Wicklow Hills to the hidden secrets of Ireland; from the outermost extremities (Sheep's Head Peninsula, West Cork) to the very heart of the country (the Westmeath forests, the canal-threaded plains of the Midlands); from places famed for drama and beauty (Connemara, Wicklow, Antrim Coast) to the places walkers seldom bother with – County Longford, County Offaly, the sort of pleasant-enough-but-unremarkable countryside you hare through on the way to somewhere sexier, without troubling to turn aside and find out what's waiting there to be discovered in the woods, fields and boglands. Some of these walks explore the heart of wonderful cities such as Dublin and Cork; some offer Dublin-dwellers an escape to the nearby delights of the Hill of Howth, the extraordinary man-made Bray–Greystones coast path, the Dublin Mountains and the Wicklow Hills.

These are stories of real walks with real people in real weather – pouring rain on the Cooley Peninsula and on Croaghan in County Antrim, mist in Monaghan, beautiful winter sun on the Wexford coast, and everything in between – fog, hail, thunder and snow. That's the beauty and the magic of walking in Ireland; you never know what weather the day is going to serve up – only that something different will be along in five minutes.

History

Among these walks you'll discover history (Erskine Childers running guns to Howth Harbour, Robert Emmet's speech from Green Street courthouse dock, Catalina and Sunderland flying boats surging from Lower Lough Erne to sink U-boats out in the Atlantic). There's a mass of fascinating myth – brave Oisin catching a giant wave on Rossbeigh Spit, Fionn MacCumhaill casting quoits, wild Queen Medbh and mighty Cúchulainn duking it out on the Cooley Peninsula up in County Louth. You'll visit places where legend and reality intertwine ('Father Ted's house' in the Burren included), and places where legend has settled on ancient structures, like the massive stone tomb on Slievenamuck in the Glen of Aherlow, where Diarmuid and Gráinne made love – but then, where didn't they?

There's social history to be read in the landscape – Wynne's Folly at Glenbeigh, built by the landlord to please his wife, but paid for by his tenants; Mount Stewart, the superbly preserved County Down house and garden of Lord and Lady Londonderry, where eccentric fantasy was let run wild through the grounds; the sprawling ruin of Downhill on the north Derry cliffs, fabulous mansion of the rather naughty Frederick Hervey, 4th Earl of Bristol and Bishop of Londonderry. Some memories have sunk forgotten back into the countryside – the famine fields, booley houses and flax pits swallowed up in Mullaghmeen Forest in Westmeath, a sweathouse in a bank above Arigna, a whole farming landscape enclosed by a forest at Derrylahan in south-west Roscommon. Other history you'll find preserved and celebrated – Clogher Heritage Centre, County Mayo, with its working forge and thatched cottage complete with butter churns and the 'hag's bed'; the Arigna Mining Experience, where former coal miners show you through the subterranean tunnels where they hewed; the vast iron stirabout cauldron of the Famine Pot, in its stone shelter near Harvey's Point in south-east Donegal.

Tradition

Ireland's countryside is a stronghold of tradition. These walks take you to holy wells, Mass Rocks, and the long, slim footprint of St Patrick blazoned on a rock. They uncover vanished ways of life that were vigorous only a generation or so ago: old hayfields, barns and mills, a potato-digging machine in an abandoned farmstead in the Sperrins, working waterways in retirement such as the Grand Canal at Tullamore, the Errina

Canal on the Shannon and the River Barrow at Carlow, their bridge abutments still indented with the grooves cut by the barge ropes. Some traditions are still a part of everyday life: currach fishing in Connemara and Clare, turf cutting by hand in Longford and Meath. That's where you'll find a good slow atmosphere, and music wherever you go, if you just look for it – at the Small Bridge in Dingle, say, or An Spailpín Fánach in the heart of Cork.

Wildlife

As for wildlife – here are red deer at Glenveagh, Irish hares in the Burren. Bird life is abundant (don't forget your binoculars): kittiwakes in Kerry, winter waders on the Wexford tideline, the liquid 'cut-price nightingale' of a blackcap on Girley Bog in Meath; a beautiful white hen harrier on the slopes of Sliabh an Iarainn, pale-bellied brent geese in Strangford Lough, a young golden eagle soaring over the Blue Stack Mountains of Donegal. Ireland's wild flowers are sensational (don't forget your flower book). The Burren region of County Clare is the cream of the crop – many species of orchid, the porcelain cups of mountain avens, the episcopal purple of bloody cranesbill; and rarities such as the white spiral of autumn lady's tresses, delicate and beautiful, or acid-loving Irish saxifrage growing in the lime-rich rock pavement. Elsewhere you'll admire rare plants such as Fox's Cabbage that you'll only find in south-west Ireland; harebells, pyramidal orchids and insectivorous butterwort on the lime-rich machair of the Low Rosses sandspit on Drumcliff Bay; Rose of Sharon with plump blackberries beside the Errina Canal in County Clare. And of course you can snack for free on wild strawberries, on the banks of the Grand Canal in Offaly, and up on the Ridge of Capard in the Slieve Bloom Mountains where the humble and commonplace broom seems to blaze a brighter gold than anywhere else in Ireland.

Scenery

Finally, the scenery and the fantastic, heart-stopping views. The walks here will take you to some of the finest in the island, views you'll never forget. There are views of mountains: Carrantuohil, Ireland's highest mountain, above the huge hanging valley of the Coomloughra Horseshoe; the magnificent north face of the Galtees from Slievenamuck in the Glen of Aherlow; magical Mullaghmore and its offshoot Sliabh Rua, twisting like fairground waltzers in the south-east corner of the Burren; Knocknarea and Benbulben from the Low Rosses in Yeats Country; the grooved dome of Knocklayd from the forest track under Croaghan, County Antrim. There are views *from* mountains: looking down on Lough Coumduala from the spine of Knockanaffrin in the Comeraghs; from Diamond Hill round the Connemara compass of coasts and islands; from Slieve Gullion, 100 miles including Carlingford Lough, the Mountains of Mourne, Slemish and the hills of Antrim, the Sperrins, Lough Neagh, Monaghan and Cavan, the vast Midland plain and the Wicklow Mountains. And one mountain above all seems to figure in many views, the shapely, free-standing bulk of Sliabh na mBan, the Mountain of the Women.

Memorable lakes include the Upper and Lower Lakes at Glendalough from the rim of the Spinc cliffs 1,000 feet overhead; the lime-powdered, brilliant turquoise turloughs or seasonal lakes of the Burren; the glacial lakes of Cavan and Monaghan. Along the Mayo coast you'll gasp over the prospect out to the Stags of Broadhaven and Benwee Head from the cliffs behind Carrowteige; in Connemara it's the subtleties of Trá Mhóir at Bunowen, where cattle munch seaweed and everyday things assume fantastic, almost psychedelic colours – white cottage, black pier, red and blue trawlers, jade-green sea, orange seaweed.

There are the great bogs with their rich smells, frogs, orchids, lousewort, bog asphodel, peregrines – and a sense of real loneliness, of peace and quiet. There are woods and forests packed in spring with wood anemones, primroses and bluebells; great rivers, like the mighty Shannon where Limerick looks across at Clare; islands, waterfalls, strange nooks and crannies. All are here, waiting for you.

Everybody's doing it

Country walking is the fastest-growing recreational activity in Europe. Not yomping along the side of a main road in wobbly shorts with iPod plugged in and grim expression plastered on, hoping to shift a couple of kilos between lunch and tea, but the kind of wandering, exploring, independent walking that puts you in touch with the countryside and opens you up to nature. 'There's a flowery lane, and a hill beyond with an old castle on top – let's go and have a look' – that kind of walking. We all crave a sniff of fresh air and a dash of the wild, and walking's the best way to get it. It's companionable, healthy, hugely enjoyable, and free. Everybody's doing it – but not in Ireland, not yet.

Of all European countries, mainland Britain is exceptionally lucky in its paths, its access laws and its maps. The paths are everywhere, a great interconnecting mesh from which you can make up your own circular walks as you please. In England and Wales most of the paths are rights of way, clearly waymarked on the ground, and they're all marked on the Ordnance Survey maps – especially the Ordnance Survey 'Explorer' 1:25,000 scale maps. In Scotland you can wander just about anywhere you please, as you can on all the high and wild land of England and Wales. The walkers of several other European countries – France, Germany, parts of Italy, Switzerland, Austria and more – also enjoy paths with legal access, waymarking and mapping when they're at home. All these keen walkers look across at Ireland, so famously green and hospitable, with her manageable mountains, beckoning hills, tangled lanes and bosky woods, and they rub their hands in anticipation. Then they come to Ireland, one of the best-endowed countries in the world for walking, yet one of the least explored on foot, and ask in bafflement – where are all the walks? It's a question the Irish themselves have been asking, with ever-increasing frustration, while the country walking revolution has been going on without them.

No right of way

Historically, Ireland has been wonderfully rich in countryside suitable for walking and hiking, but extremely poorly provided with public rights of way. A background of landlord ownership (often absentee) and dependent tenants who felt unable to stand up for their rights produced a situation where most people had access to paths across private land only on sufferance of the landowner, who could withdraw permission at any time. By the turn of the 20th century the tenants had bought out the landlords. But the last thing these newly independent small farmers wanted to do was to open up their hard-won land to the general public. So the paths remained open on sufferance, and legal rights of way stayed few and far between. That is largely still the case today, and it explains why the Irish Ordnance Survey maps show so few rights of way, and why many farmers and landowners are still unaccustomed to strangers walking on their land. There's generally a presumption of access on mountains, moors and uplands, by way of time-hallowed routes. But even these can still be closed at any time by a landowner's whim.

Maps

A big problem here – Ordnance Survey of Ireland (OSI) and Ordnance Survey of Northern Ireland (OSNI) only cover their respective sectors of the island at a scale of 1:50,000, and – for reasons explained above – the maps show very few rights of way. Walker-friendly maps at 1:25,000 are rarer than hens' teeth. So far, OSI (www.osi.ie) only offer the Aran Islands, Killarney National Park and a couple of other locations in the Republic. Ordnance Survey of Northern Ireland produces a series of five Activity Maps at 1:25,000 – Strangford Lough, Sperrins, Glens of Antrim, Lough Erne and Mourne Mountains. Visit https://maps. osni.gov.uk/SearchResults.aspx?SearchCat=Activity%20Maps.

Other walking maps: you can get hold of East–West Mapping's 1:30,000 maps of the Dublin and Wicklow Mountains, or Tim Robinson's wonderfully detailed 'Folding Landscape' maps of

Connemara, The Burren and the Aran Islands at 1, 2 and 2.2 inches to the mile respectively. But that's about it. This is a parlous situation, which will be remedied as and when more people walk more widely in Ireland.

So – where do you start on finding out where you'll be welcome to walk?

Looped Walks and Quality Walks

In the last few years, serious efforts have been made on both sides of the border to cater for walkers. By far the most significant recent development for ordinary country walkers in the Republic has been the establishment of more than 250 (and counting) National Looped Walks by the Republic's domestic tourist organisation Fáilte Ireland and the Department of Community, Rural and Gaeltacht Affairs, working with the national forestry organisation Coillte. These Looped Walks emanate out from designated trailheads, and they range from easy strolls to tough mountain hikes. You'll find them all across Ireland, on land privately and publicly owned, on farmland, coasts and hills, in woodlands and in the mountains. You can walk them with complete confidence that you will be welcome. The recently introduced Walks Scheme – essentially a grant to landowners, encouraging them to maintain their paths and welcome walkers – has been hugely beneficial in opening up the Looped Walks. They are generally half a day's worth; they are well maintained, clearly waymarked, and downloadable in the form of printable instructions and maps (www. discoverireland.ie/walking). In Northern Ireland the Quality Walks fulfil the same function (www.walkni.com). Most of the walks in this book are based either on Looped Walks or Quality Walks so, very unusually for a collection of Irish walks, you can be sure you're in no danger of being turned away from any of them.

National Waymarked Ways

Longer established are the National Waymarked Ways, a collection of 40 long-distance routes of varying lengths, some of several days' or weeks' duration, all across the Republic. A full list is at http://www.irishtrails.ie/National_Waymarked_Trails/. Examples range from the six-day Wicklow Way through the Wicklow Mountains near Dublin to the ten-day Dingle Way out in western County Kerry, and from the dead flat Grand Canal Way through the Midlands to the wild and woolly Western Way that runs 250 km/155 miles through Mayo and Galway.

Until recently Northern Ireland boasted only one long-distance path, a 950 km/600 mile loop called the Ulster Way. It was too long, mostly on roads, and badly maintained and waymarked. Now it has been relaunched in 16 'Quality Sections' under different names (e.g. Ring of Gullion Way through South Armagh, Causeway Coast Way along the spectacular Antrim Coast, Mourne Way through the Mourne Mountains) which are joined up by 'linked sections' to form one mighty trail round the whole Province (details at http://www.walkni.com/ulsterway/).

These Waymarked Ways are great alternatives to the Looped Walks and Quality Walks for any walker who wants to spend several days afoot and get to know a stretch of varied country. A word of warning, though: some have been better maintained than others, so don't expect a featherbed experience on every Waymarked Way. They suit self-reliant walkers who enjoy both rough and smooth, and can look after themselves and use a map/compass/GPS if need be.

National Trails Day is in October (www.nationaltrailsday.ie). This website contains loads of trails: http://www.irishtrails.ie/trails.aspx?c=-1&t=-1.

Walking clubs

Given the history and the lack of legal rights of way, it's no surprise to find both the Republic and the North full of thriving, dedicated, knowledgeable local walking clubs. They are mostly based on the beautiful, easily accessible mountain and hill ranges that lie scattered all across the island. I've been amazed to find out how many clubs there are – one in almost every local town. In a country with few rights of way, there's help, advice and confidence in numbers; and in walking with people who know the fields and woods, and the individual farmers and landowners who live and work among them. Many local clubs organise regular walks on specific days; they put on family days, challenge walks, sponsored hikes, specialist interest walks and so on. These clubs, without exception, are delighted to have visiting walkers along and introduce them to the countryside they so clearly know and love. So don't be shy!

The Irish Heart Foundation (www.irishheart.ie) lists around 70 walking clubs in the Republic, and the Ulster Federation of Rambling Clubs (www.ufrc-online.co.uk) can put you in touch with over 30 member walking clubs in Northern Ireland. Or consult the local Tourist Information Office.

Local walking clubs I have personally found wonderful are:

- Slieve Bloom Walking Club, Cos Offaly and Laois (www.
  slievebloom.ie; www.offaly.ie/offalyhome/visitoffaly/Active/
  Walking/The+Eco-Walks): guided walks on Sundays
  (http://www.slievebloom.ie/walking_programme.html;
  086-278-9147)
- Tinahely Walking Club, South Wicklow (Margaret
  Coogan, 087-2852997, kylefarm@eircom.net): Sundays in
  the summer
- Ballyhoura Bears, Limerick/Cork/Tipperary (www.
  ballyhourabears.com)
- Glen of Aherlow Fáilte Society, Tipperary (www.aherlow.
  com)
- Boherquill Ramblers, Westmeath (www.irelandwalking.ie)
- Ballyvaughan Fanore Walking Club, The Burren, Co Clare
  (www.ballyvaughanfanorewalkingclub.com)
- Bailieborough local walks, Co Cavan (John Ed Sheanon,
  042-966-5342): Wednesday evenings
- Peaks Mountaineering Club, Clonmel, Tipperary (www.
  clonmelhillwalking.org): Sunday walks and more

Walking festivals

Walking festivals are hugely popular; a chance to walk
somewhere you don't know with like-minded people, guided
by locals who are keen to share all the best walks and special
places. Walks are graded, so there's something for both the
lily-livered and the hairy-chested. Conversation, craic and a
party mood are guaranteed.

For a list of walking festivals in the Republic: http://www.discoverireland.com/us/search/?q=walking+festivals.

For festivals in Northern Ireland: http://www.walkni.com/FantasticFestivals.aspx.

Some great ones are:

- Limerick, Cork – Ballyhoura Walking Festival, April/May: www.ballyhouracountry.com
- Tipperary, Limerick – Glen of Aherlow Walking Festivals, Winter (late Jan) and Summer (June Bank Holiday): www.aherlow.ie
- Waterford – Dunmore East Rambling Weekend, May: www.dunmorewalks.com
- West Cork – West Cork Walking Festival, September
- Westmeath – Midlands International Walking Festival, May: www.irelandwalking.ie
- Laois, Offaly – Slieve Bloom Walking Festival, May; and Slieve Bloom Eco Walks Festival, September: www.slievebloom.ie
- Clare – Burren Peaks Walking Festival, September: www.burrenpeakswalkingfestival.com
- Wexford – Askamore Walking Festival, June Bank Holiday: obrien.sean3@gmail.com (087-254-5739)
- Wicklow – Tinahely Trail Walking Festival, April: www.tinahely.ie
- Leitrim – Sliabh an Iarainn Walking Festival, September: leitrimwalks@gmail.com
- Waterford/Tipperary – Knockmealdown Crossing Mountain Challenge, April (18.5 miles, 8 hours, tough challenge): www.peaksmcclonmel.ie

Other sources of great walks

All the organisations below are keen to spread the word about walking, and can help with advice and contacts:

- The Ramblers (NI): www.ramblers.org.uk
- Walking Ireland: www.walkingireland.ie
- Keep Ireland Open: www.keepirelandopen.org
- An Óige (Irish Youth Hostel Association): www.anoige.ie
- Walking In Ireland: www.walkinginireland.org
- Mountaineering Ireland: www.mountaineeringireland.ie
- Walkers Association of Ireland: www.walkersassociation.ie

Irish Independent's Walk of the Week

I would say that, wouldn't I? Every Saturday, in the Travel Section of the *Irish Independent*.

Have a wonderful walk – have 50!

Do get in touch with me through csomerville@independent.ie, or via my website www.christophersomerville.co.uk – I'm always delighted to discuss old routes, or hear about new ones, or just swap news and gossip about these glorious walks.

1

DINGLE WAY: ANASCAUL TO DINGLE, CO KERRY

A BLOWY, BLUSTERY WEST Kerry day, a dozen miles of the Dingle Way to cover, and who better to tackle them with than John Ahern of South West Walks Ireland? I couldn't have wished for a more vigorous or conversational companion on a day when the north wind seemed determined to drive blacker and blacker clouds of wetter and wetter content in over the Dingle Peninsula's mountains and out again across Dingle Bay.

Mind you, the drenchings we got would have been laughed to scorn, if he had even registered them, by the man whose name was lettered along the front of the South Pole Inn in Anascaul. Thomas Crean was a hard, hard man. As a teenager in the 1890s he ran away from Anascaul to join the Navy. He accompanied Captain Scott on two of his famous Antarctic expeditions, including the doomed journey of 1910–12. He voyaged 800 miles with Ernest Shackleton in an open boat through the Southern Ocean in a bid to fetch help for colleagues trapped by pack ice. Then he came home to Anascaul and ran the pub, spinning tales across the counter until his death in 1938, having reached the age of 61 against all the odds.

Dark blocks of rain dragging fragments of rainbow in their skirts melted into brief windows of intense sunshine, making the gorse hedges glow sulphurously and the bushes of may shine blindingly white. Down on the southern shore we passed the grim tower of Minard Castle – a Fitzgerald stronghold blown to ruins in the 1650s by Oliver Cromwell's men, said John. Gannets were planing over Dingle Bay on black-tipped wings, toppling over to plunge into the rain-pocked sea after fish. On the far shore of the bay rose the mountain ridges of the Iveragh Peninsula, far higher and more sharply cut than Dingle's smoothly undulating backbone.

Beyond the castle, hidden in a leafy dingle, we found a beautiful horseshoe of grass enclosing Tobar Eoin. Offerings of coins and bright white quartz chips lay at the bottom of the holy well. The gently dimpling water was cool on my wind-roughened lips, sweet on the palate. Good for the eyes, too, John told me. Above the well a seamed old tree had been festooned with strips of rag, each tied there for a wish or a prayer.

Narrow country lanes led us on westward, climbing into the foothills of the mountains past abandoned farms where trees flourished in the derelict rooms. John beguiled the showers and the miles with a rich outpouring of talk. For a short while we followed the line of the old Tralee & Dingle Light Railway. This rickety-rackety branch line, closed with much mourning in 1953, was a wonder and a wild amusement to legions of enthusiasts. The fireman's duties included pelting coal lumps at sheep straying on the line. You could run from Tralee to Dingle more swiftly than the trains would trundle. 'It was a nice question,' said John, 'as to who took on more liquid refreshment at Camp Junction – the engine or the guard! Oh, a great institution, and a great source of crack.'

Now the Dingle Way left the lanes and climbed up to cross the slopes of Cruach Sceirde, the Scattered Mountain. The stones of ancient huts and field walls patterned the brown turf. We climbed above small mountain farms to a high pass in the teeth of wind and rain. Below in a hollow of the coast the circle of Dingle Harbour lay cradled. A beautiful pale sunset layered the sea beyond with pure silver. A long gleaming ribbon of laneway led us down out of the rainy hills, into the town where strangers and friends seem two sides of the same coin.

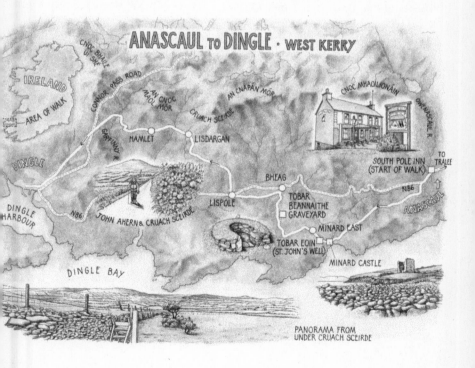

WAY TO GO

MAP: OS of Ireland 1:50,000 Discovery 70.

TRAVEL: N22 to Tralee; N86 to Dingle; bus service 275 to Anascaul.

WALK DIRECTIONS: (NB Dingle Way / DW is waymarked with yellow 'walking man' symbols and arrows): From South Pole Inn, Anascaul (OS ref 593019), cross river. 200 m up Dingle road, left (DW) along Castlemaine road. Left along R561 (589013); in 150 m, right up lane for 3 miles to Minard Castle (555992). Ahead up lane; in 50 m fork right (DW) up grassy track (Tobar Eoin in front of you here). Continue through Minard East (549997); in ¼ mile, left (545999 – DW) for ½ mile to T-junction. Right (539995 – DW) for ¾ mile, passing Tobar Beannaithe graveyard (537003). Right at top of hill (536006 – DW). At T-junction (DW), left into Bheag.

On right bend, left (538012 – DW) for 1⅓ miles to join N86 in Lispole (519010). Forward across bridge; immediately right up lane. At fork (517018 – DW), left on lane; right into fields after 1 mile (502024 – DW) – NB *Not* where OS map shows it at 510022!

Up three fields; then left (503028 – DW) to road. Forward through Lisdargan to junction (501031 – DW). Right; in 50 m, left (DW) along green lane. In 300 m, left (DW), over fields (DW; stiles) to road (488032). In 200 m right (DW) across fields to road (482032). Continue to pass a house; in 50 m, right (479031 – yellow arrow) up track, following DW up mountainside for ⅔ mile to cross Garfinny River and reach road (474038). Left for 2 miles into Dingle.

LENGTH: 12 miles: allow 6–7 hours.

GRADE: Moderate

CONDITIONS: Don't forget your raingear and good boots.

DON'T MISS:
- Minard Castle
- Tobar Eoin
- a session in the Small Bridge pub, Dingle

REFRESHMENTS: None en route – take a picnic.

INFORMATION: *Tourist Office:* Dingle Tourist Office, Strand Street, Dingle; 066-915-1188; www.discoverireland.ie/southwest.

Dingle Way guide books/leaflets: From Dingle Tourist Office.

Southwestwalks Ireland: 066-71-28733; www.southwestwalksireland.com.

2

WINDY GAP, IVERAGH PENINSULA, CO KERRY

'WE ARE WET OUTSIDES and we are wet insides,' grinned the two flaxen-haired German girls in the lane outside Glenbeigh. Their sopping waterproofs, quite patently, were nothing of the sort. Sean O'Suilleabhain and I nodded back sympathetically as the latest of this day's downpours bounced off our backs.

It had certainly been a bloody old summer, all right. But I would have braved far worse than a bit of a soaking for the chance to cross Windy Gap with the self-effacing gentleman whom Lady Fortune had put in my way today. If you're lucky enough to have Sean O'Suilleabhain as a walking companion through County Kerry, then you're lucky indeed. This modest and gently humorous man, the founding father of the Kerry Way long-distance footpath, is a fountain of fact and fiction concerning his beloved native county.

Gale force winds were forecast to sweep in across the Iveragh Mountains, dragging much of the Atlantic in their skirts. In the event we beat them to it, and were rewarded by some of the finest far prospects in Ireland, a full palette of subtle colour and vigorous movement – mountains smoking with cloud and rain, foothills and shores muted into slaty shades of blue and grey, the sea a mass of curved white shark's teeth as it surged landward through the channels and sandspits of Dingle Bay.

The stark shell of Glenbeigh Tower stood a field away as we started along the lane. 'Wynne's Folly,' murmured Sean. 'Built by Lord Headley Wynne in the 1860s to please his wife, and paid for by increasing the rents of his tenants. Those who couldn't  find the extra money were evicted.' He sighed. 'A familiar story, and a scandal which reached the House of Commons.'

From the zigzag path up to Windy Gap we looked back west where the whaleback of Rossbeigh Hill, dull gold in its coat of wet gorse flowers, framed the long promontory of Rossbeigh Spit reaching out across the mouth of Castlemaine Harbour towards the spit of Inch. 'Oisin caught his giant wave there on Rossbeigh Spit, and surfed it on out to Tir na nOg,' said Sean. Wind-driven rollers broke in spray on the twin opposing strands as we watched, not quite mighty enough to transport a hero, perhaps, but a fine sight nonetheless.

It was windy at Windy Gap, a good shoving half-gale that got well behind us and pushed us on down a wide stony track – the old main road from once-populous Glencar out to the coast and the church at Glenbeigh, Sean told me. I had eyes only for the forward view now, a stunning prospect over Lough Caragh lying quiet and sheltered in its dreamy wooded valley, brushed by bands of sun-silvered rain. All round the valley rose a protective ring of mountains. Sean ran his eyes along their flanks and ridges like a man counting treasure.

Up ahead beyond the lake stood the huge hanging valley of the Coomloughra Horseshoe, dark and thunderous under the cloud-obscured peak of Carrantuohil. 'Ireland's highest mountain at 3,406 feet,' observed my companion, 'and I used to take schoolfriends up there as a kid from my uncle's house in the Brida Valley. That's where I must have got my love of walking and the outdoors from, but I really didn't know what I was doing back then. I couldn't even read a map and compass! Somehow I survived, though.'

Indeed he did. Lovers of County Kerry's great wild spaces owe a huge debt to Sean O'Suilleabhain and his fellow walkers, who have kept so many old green roads open with such persistence and energy. Coming off the mountainside and down the road under the wrinkled flanks of Commaun towards the tumbling sea in Dingle Bay, I smiled to myself at the thought that there might still be heroes in Kerry after all.

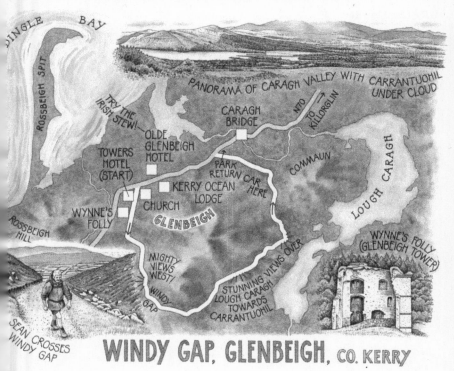

WINDY GAP, GLENBEIGH, CO. KERRY

WAY TO GO

MAP: OS of Ireland 1:50,000 Discovery 78; downloadable map/instructions at http://tcs.ireland.ie/dataland/TCSAttachments/341_TheKerryWay.pdf.

TRAVEL:

N70 from Tralee or N72 from Killarney to Killorglin; N70 to Glenbeigh. For two-car walkers, park one car neatly up side road off N70, ¼ mile west of Caragh Bridge, and drive other car on for ¾ mile into Glenbeigh. Park near Towers Hotel in Main Street.

WALK DIRECTIONS: By Towers Hotel turn up road past church (Kerry Way/KW 'walking man' waymark post). In ⅓ mile take first lane on left (KW). Follow KW to end of tarmac, then up track to cross Windy Gap and descend to three-way finger-post. Keep ahead ('Scenic Route') to reach road and follow it down to N70 and return car near Caragh Bridge.

LENGTH: 6 miles: allow 3 hours.

GRADE: Moderate

CONDITIONS: Good tracks and country roads.

DON'T MISS:
- ruin of Wynne's Folly
- wonderful views over Dingle Bay from Windy Gap
- stunning vista of Caragh Valley and Lough, backed by Carrantuohil, from old road beyond Windy Gap

REFRESHMENTS: Olde Glenbeigh Hotel (066-976-8333; www.glenbeighhotel. com) – real home cooking.

INFORMATION:

Tourist Office: Iveragh Road, Killorglin; 066-976-1451; http://www.discoverireland. ie/Southwest.aspx.

The Kerry Way by Sandra Bardwell (Rucksack Readers).

Go Ireland (066-976-2094; www.govisitireland.com) offer guided walks.

3

MUCKROSS LAKE AND TORC WATERFALL, KILLARNEY NATIONAL PARK, CO KERRY

GIVEN THE HUNDREDS OF thousands of sightseers who throng into Killarney National Park every year, it's really remarkable how those wonderful lakes and mountains of County Kerry have retained their tranquil beauty, the air of peace and quiet that so attracted Victorian adventurers.

On a brisk afternoon between winter and spring I set out 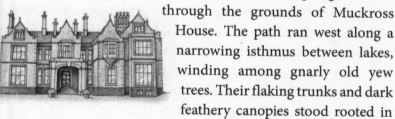 through the grounds of Muckross House. The path ran west along a narrowing isthmus between lakes, winding among gnarly old yew trees. Their flaking trunks and dark feathery canopies stood rooted in banks of rock cloaked in damp green moss and sprouting ferns.

A gleam of water on my left hand, and suddenly Muckross Lake lay spread in all its glory, sparkling as if a million diamonds had been strewn there. Lough Leane opened on the right, as big as a sea inlet by comparison, with a ridge of mountains far away on the northern skyline – Slieve Mish, the backbone of the Dingle Peninsula some 15 miles off.

Where the two lakes flowed together I crossed the narrows by a humpy bridge, then rounded the west end of Muckross Lake beside reedbeds glowing pale gold in the mid-afternoon sun. Cheerful voices came from the tea-garden at Dinis Cottage where a group of young doctors had just arrived on foot, desperate for tea and flapjacks. Luckily  for them, and for me, the little café had just returned to life after its winter closure. I got a pot of tea and a piece of damp, glutinous brack, and took them to a table by the window. The view over the lake was curiously blurred. I rubbed my glasses, then the window, trying in vain to get rid of the misty effect. Dozens of signatures, cartoons and *bons mots* had been scratched by visitors into the panes with diamond rings over the course of two centuries.

J.D. Hogg's signature, dated 1816, was the oldest I could find. I wondered if a rather abrupt 'Wellesley' had been the Duke of Wellington's handiwork. One couldn't help speculating on the vanished signatories. What of 'Lizzie' and 'The Doctor', who enclosed their names in 1856 within the outline of a love-apple? Spooners, honeymooners, or just good friends?

Walking on east along the south shore of the lake and picturing Lizzie (freckled, pert, inclined to tease) and The Doctor (twinkly, bespectacled, rather older than her), the miles sped by. I was at the foot of the steep zigzag path to Torc Waterfall before I knew it. I climbed quickly against the fading light, looping up and then sharply down with the whispery echo of the fall growing nearer. The water sluiced down a dark mossy channel, in creamy skeins as delicate and lacy as a

Shetland shawl, turning once before crashing down into a pool in a rainbow mist. A damp breath stole from the fall, a rich scent of wet leaves and moss.

A young couple sat motionless and silent on the brink of the pool. His arm was round her waist, her hand was on his knee. They were entirely bound up in each other, in the falling water and in the moment. A happy man and woman. I hope Lizzie and The Doctor found such happiness among the Killarney mountains.

WAY TO GO

MAP: OS of Ireland 1:50,000 Discovery 78; Muckross Estate map from Killarney National Park Visitor Centre, Muckross House.

Downloadable map/instructions (recommended) at www.discoverireland.ie/walking.

TRAVEL:

Rail (www.irishrail.ie) to Killarney; jaunting car (haggle your price) or bus (www. buseireann.ie) to Muckross.

Road: N71 from Killarney towards Kenmare; Muckross House signed on right in 3 miles. Free car park.

WALK DIRECTIONS: Leaving Muckross House, ahead along avenue; left in 250 yards ('Dinis Cottage'). Follow track for 2½ miles around Muckross Lake to Dinis Cottage tearooms. (Meeting of the Waters: down steps beyond lavatory block.) Continue along surfaced track for ¾ mile to N71 Killarney–Kenmare road. Bear right to cross (take care!); follow gravel track (yellow, blue, red trail arrows; 'Muckross House' fingerpost). In ½ mile descend to road.

(a) Return to Muckross House: cross road, follow path ('Muckross House').

(b) For Torc Waterfall (steep up and down, many steps): don't cross road, but bear uphill (ignore 'Torc Waterfall' arrow pointing other way!) on good path, steep in parts. Path zigzags, then levels out; take left fork (coloured arrows here point back the way you've come!) to cross Owengarriff River. In 25 yards, left (ignore arrows and 'Kerry Way' sign), following path directly above right (east) bank of river. Path soon slopes and steepens down steps to Torc Waterfall.

Continue down path to cross N71. Through gap in fence; left along path; in 50 yards, right ('Muckross House 1.8 km') to return to car park.

LENGTH: 5½ miles around Muckross Lake (easy; allow 2 hours); 7 miles including Torc Waterfall (moderate; allow 3-4 hours).

CONDITIONS: Well surfaced paths. Torc Waterfall extension: steep ascent, steep descent with many steps. Dog-friendly (on leads, please).

DON'T MISS:
- lake views from north side
- window graffiti in Dinas Cottage
- Torc waterfall

MUCKROSS LAKE AND TORC WATERFALL

REFRESHMENTS: Dinis Cottage tearoom, Muckross House restaurant/café (064-31440).

INFORMATION:

Tourist Information Office: Beech Road, Killarney; 064-31633; www.discoverireland.ie.

Muckross House: 064-31440; www.muckross-house.ie.

National Parks: www.npws.ie.

27

4

LIGHTHOUSE LOOP,
SHEEP'S HEAD
PENINSULA, CO CORK

AHOY, AND GOOD MORNING! At last I was here, where I'd promised myself I'd one day be – out at the tip of the Sheep's Head Peninsula under a pink and grey sky, with a strong sea breeze blowing in over West Cork, a dark sea full of whitecaps, and the Atlantic seething up against the cliffs as if it would hiss and thump them to bits.

Sheep's Head is wild. It's rough, and it's windy. The view south from the Sheep's Head Café was spectacular as I started my walk, out to the Mizen hills across Dunmanus Bay. But when I'd slipped and slid across the rocks and heather to a viewpoint over the polished, jet-black ellipse of Lough Akeen, I found that the lift of the land had been hiding an even more jaw-dropping prospect northwards – the sleeping whale shape of Bear Island with the great hummocks of Slieve Miskish and the Caha Mountains beyond, forming the dinosaur spine of the Beara Peninsula, all a dark purple bruise against the scudding grey sky.

The sea and land panorama from above Lough Akeen must really be one of the finest in all Ireland. Even Jimmy Tobin, who has been farming these hill slopes for more years than he cares to count, leaned on his stick and gazed around in appreciation at a view he must have seen ten thousand times. Jimmy is one of the many dozens of farmers all over Ireland who are taking part in the Walks Scheme, a programme which sees its participants looking after the footpaths and welcoming the walkers that cross their land. 'We like to see people out and about on Sheep's Head,' Jimmy remarked as we followed his sheepdog Jojo down through the rocks, 'it keeps the old paths walked and brings a bit of life to the place.'

The outer tip of Sheep's Head is a boggy bit of ground. Frogs were burping and grunting in the marshy hollows, too intent on mating to look out for their natural enemies. Jimmy pointed out a sinuating track through the water plants left by an otter who had sneaked up unnoticed on the plump pairs of ranine lovers. We squelched on down to climb the steps to the stumpy lighthouse, built in 1968 to warn oil tankers bound for Whiddy Island off the rocks and reefs of Rinn Mhuintir Bháire. 'There was a power of work in these steps,' murmured Jimmy. He should know – he built them.

Along the north coast of Sheep's Head the path grew progressively wilder, emerging from a deep defile to run along the very rim of sheer cliffs that plunged past kittiwake ledges to a yeasty, milky green sea. 'See that big flagstone down there?' Jimmy pointed to a black, sea-smoothed rock platform far below, rhythmically washed by the waves. 'My father would fish off there with a mussel on the hook. No rod, just a big old stick.'

We slithered across red rocks banded white with quartz, and teetered over pools by way of rough stepping stones. Turning our backs on Beara, we made inland towards the café through a jigsaw of small stone-walled fields. Jimmy showed me an ancient milling stone, cross-hatched and holed through the middle, hidden in the stones of a wall. Here had been houses, potato ridges, barns, crops. 'A family lived in it until the 1950s. Lonely? Wasn't it, though? And no road at all, just a foot track over the mountain.'

He gestured to the overgrown square of a tiny hayfield. 'I last took a cut of hay out of that with a scythe when I was 15, and carried it back to the house barefoot. That was the way of it,' said Jimmy, half to himself, 'and we weren't any the worse.'

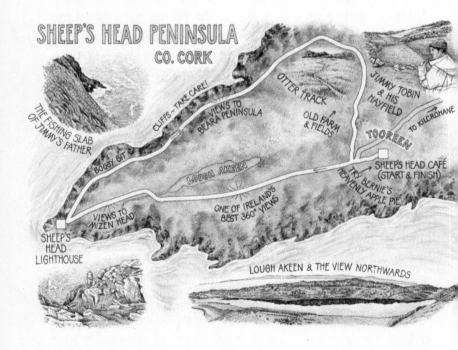

SHEEP'S HEAD PENINSULA

CO. CORK

THE FISHING SLAB OF JIMMY'S FATHER

CLIFFS – TAKE CARE!

VIEWS TO BEARA PENINSULA

OTTER TRACK

OLD FARM & FIELDS

JIMMY TOBIN & HIS HAYFIELD

TO KILCROHANE

TOOREEN

BOGGY BIT

LOUGH AKEEN

TRY BERNIE'S HEAVENLY APPLE PIE

SHEEP'S HEAD CAFÉ (START & FINISH)

VIEWS TO MIZEN HEAD

ONE OF IRELAND'S BEST 360° VIEWS

SHEEP'S HEAD LIGHTHOUSE

LOUGH AKEEN & THE VIEW NORTHWARDS

WAY TO GO

MAP: OS of Ireland 1:50,000 Discovery 88; downloadable map/instructions at www. discoverireland.ie/walking.

TRAVEL:

Bus (www.buseireann.ie): Service 255 (Saturday only) from Macroom and Bantry to Kilcrohane.

Road: N71 Bantry towards Ballydehob; R591 to Durrus; minor road signed to Ahakista, Kilcrohane and Tooreen (Sheep's Head Café).

WALK DIRECTIONS (follow blue arrows): From Sheep's Head Café, ahead down road, then path. Cross lower end of Lough Akeen; follow 'lighthouse' sign past helicopter pad to lighthouse. Return and pass along left side of green stores container; continue along valley, then north coast cliffs for 1 mile to marker post with blue arrow pointing right. Aim for post above; follow rough waymark boards and orange/yellow waymarkers back to café.

LENGTH: 2½ miles: allow 2–3 hours.

GRADE: Moderate

CONDITIONS: Some boggy bits; slippery paths near unguarded cliff edge – keep kids and dogs under control.

DON'T MISS:
- panoramic view over Lough Akeen
- Sheep's Head lighthouse
- Sheep's Head Café's apple pie, fresh-baked by Bernie Tobin

REFRESHMENTS: Sheep's Head Café (027-67878), open April–September, 11–6 daily.

INFORMATION:

Bantry Tourist Office: The Square, Bantry; 027-50229; www.westcork.ie.

A Guide to the Sheep's Head Way by Tom Whitty (available locally).

www.thesheepsheadway.ie.

5

Slí an Easa, Guagán Barra Forest Park, Co Cork

'WELL, AFTER RAIN LIKE we had last night,' said Neil Lucey as he waved us off from the steps of Gougane Barra Hotel, 'I'd recommend Slí an Easa, the Waterfall Trail.' He held out a palm to gauge the spitting wind, and gave a grin. 'It should be roaring up there, all right!'

Gougane Barra Hotel, perched beside Guagán Barra Lake in north-west Cork, is a well-found vessel of hospitality and comfort, helmed by the Cronin/Lucey family through five generations. Its current boss is nothing if not positive and forward-thinking. Coillte (Ireland's forestry authority) have gone a long way to make the Guagán Barra Forest Park walker-friendly, but Neil Lucey dreams of more – a network of waymarked footpaths, through and beyond the secret glen where the River Lee springs. Good news for walkers and lovers of tucked-away country, one fine day.

It certainly was roaring in the forest beyond the lake as we climbed the puddled pathways of Slí an Easa. The wind came blustering in from the west with rain swirling in its hem, causing the pines to hiss like a boiling sea as it rushed overhead from rim to rim of the glen. The woods were loud with the gush and trickle of overloaded streamlets. Mats of moss hung over the narrow rocky channels of the waterways, each feathery tendril dribbling its individual string of silver long after the rain had stopped.

A darkly glistening rosette of toothed leaves clung to a wet rock, with a solitary stalk of tiny white flowers still bravely standing tall. 'Fox's Cabbage!' exclaimed the botanist half in my wife Jane. 'What a beautiful thing,' murmured her artistic side. Both were spot on. *Saxifraga spathularis*, a shiny and heavily serrated plant of shady and well-watered places, arrived from its stronghold in the Iberian peninsula some time in the deep past before sea levels rose and isolated it in south-west Ireland, where the mild winters suit it just fine. Some call it St Patrick's Cabbage; others 'Cabáiste na ndaoine maithe', the Good People's Cabbage. Sturdy and thick, it doesn't much call the fairy folk to mind, but maybe they find the solid umbrella-like leaves a handy hiding place.

The scratchy *cheedle-cheedle-chee* of goldcrests called our gaze upwards to the treetops where a flock of the little birds was bouncing from sprig to sprig, their brilliant gold foreheads flashing against the dark green of the pines. Water vapour hung heavy in the resin-scented air, making the dried heads of foxgloves and the shamrock-shaped leaves of oxalis sag with droplets.

A flight of slippery steps led us high into the wood, where a swollen mountain stream crashed down its rocks in a spectacular cataract. We teetered across the stepping stones and went on up to a viewing platform among trees under the peak of Tuarin Beag. The whole of Guagán Barra glen lay spread out under ragged patches of blue torn by the wind in the racing grey sky. Great rock faces rose, their strata canted at steep angles. Across the valley white skeins of water twisted as they tumbled from the dark purple rim of moorland towards the lake hundreds of feet below. One day, if Neil Lucey's dreams come true, there will be more walkers among those peaks, more wanderers on the moors.

Back down by Guagán Barra Lake we crossed the short causeway to pay a call to St Finbarr's Oratory. Long before he ventured down the River Lee to found the city of Cork, fair-haired Finbarr lived on the islet in Guagán Barra Lake, a hermit alone with God among the mountains. For austere beauty and a wild grandeur of surroundings, Finbarr could not have done better. Just as well that Gougane Barra Hotel didn't exist back then – the temptation of a nice hot cup of tea might have been too much even for a copper-bottomed saint to turn his back on.

WAY TO GO

MAP: OS of Ireland 1:50,000 Discovery 85; downloadable map/instructions (highly recommended) at http://www.coillteoutdoors.ie/?id=53&rec_site=88.

TRAVEL:

Road: From Ballingeary, R584 to Guagán crossroads; right to reach Gougane Barra Hotel. From Bantry, N71 to Ballylickey; right for 15 miles to Guagán crossroads; left to hotel.

WALK DIRECTIONS: From Gougane Barra Hotel, follow lakeside road into Guagán Barra Forest Park. At first car park (NB €5 fee for cars, in coins), take track on left (Waterfall Trail/Slí an Easa). Soon cross footbridge, then track. Continue up path, zigzagging through wood to return above car park. Left up steps ('Radharc/ Viewpoint'). Cross river at waterfall (stepping stones); continue up steps to viewpoint. Return to 'Radharc/Viewpoint' sign; bear left across footbridge and fall to return to car park and lakeside road to Gougane Barra hotel. Cross causeway to visit St Finbarr's Oratory.

NB The official walk is described back-to-front here, to leave the best waterfall till last.

LENGTH: Waterfall Trail/Slí an Easa, 1¼ miles (allow 1 hour); add half an hour for there-and-back from hotel.

GRADE: Moderate/Hard

CONDITIONS: Forest tracks, many steps.

DON'T MISS:
- natural gardens of ferns, liverworts and mosses, including Fox's Cabbage
- stepping stone crossing beside the high fall
- view over Guagán Barra glen from Tuarin Beag viewpoint

OTHER WALKS: Several other waymarked trails explore Guagán Barra Forest Park.

REFRESHMENTS: Gougane Barra Hotel (026-47069; www.gouganebarrahotel. com) – welcoming, relaxing, family-run place on the lake.

INFORMATION:

Tourist Office: Old Courthouse, Bantry; 027-50229; www.discoverireland.ie/ Southwest.

6

CORK CITY,
CO CORK

CORK IS A GREAT strolling city. There's a comfortable, lived-in appearance to the winding streets and back lanes, attractive low-level Georgian houses and public buildings, handsome church towers and spires to give drama to the skyline, and a fine succession of bridges spanning the twin channels of the River Lee that part and join to make an island of much of the old city. Down on the south bank I paused to admire the space-rocket pinnacles and the sculptures of angels, saints and demons so exuberantly smothering St Fin Barre's Cathedral. Then I crossed the South Channel of the River Lee and headed into the centre of the city past the site of what was once a fountain head of pure Cork nectar – Beamish & Crawford's brewery on South Main Street. I thought of the sweet tang of Cork stout, and of a rattling good reel. 'Oh aye, there'll be a session tonight all right,' agreed the barman in the dark snug interior of An Spailpín Fánach. 'Do you play yourself? Well, you'll be welcome.'

The English Market was crammed with knicker stalls and odd-shaped second-hand book booths, and with butchers, bakers and hot-sauce makers. My breakfast consisted of a lump of Cratloe sheep's cheese in a tanner bun, a treat fit for a hero. I munched it as I wandered the narrow old lanes of the Huguenot Quarter, refuge and workplace for dozens of Protestants on the run from religious intolerance in pre-revolutionary France. Here Rory Gallagher Place honours the late rock guitarist who was brought up in Cork. Gallagher, the bluesy master of the Stratocaster, eschewed stardom's trappings; his trademark working-man's plaid shirts and battered jeans symbolised his unassuming nature. His adoptive city has raised a bold monument in Rory Gallagher Place – a sculpture of a twisted, fiery guitar with notes and lyrics streaming from it like flames.

Bell chimes were floating down on the north wind from Shandon. I crossed Christy Ring Bridge and made for the tower of St Anne's, high above the city against a blackening sky.

> On this I ponder
> Where'er I wander,
> And thus grow fonder,
> Sweet Cork, of thee,
> With thy bells of Shandon
> That sound so grand on
> The pleasant waters
> Of the River Lee.

Old Father Prout is certainly Shandon's most famous son, but he might not be exactly the most popular. His song 'The Bells of Shandon', written nearly two centuries ago, has drawn countless pilgrims to climb the tower on the hill and try to knock a tune out of the famous bells. All day, every day, local residents must grin and bear the sound of punters chancing their ringing arm on 'Amazing Grace' or 'Molly Malone'.

I had an over-confident go at 'Out on the Ocean', a jig I had temporarily on the brain. A nasty discordant mess of clangs and jangles shivered the midday quiet of the hill. I'm sorry, good folk of Shandon. Blame it on the sheep's cheese.

Back by the River Lee I passed the massive and futuristic face of Cork's Opera House. I had a cup of tea in the Crawford Art Gallery and a look at their collection of Irish Impressionists – blurry scenes packed full of nostalgia. In Rory Gallagher Place a young girl in a home-made skirt had set up to play in the shadow of the twisted Strat sculpture. She sang a Kate Rusby song in a brave little voice. Cork's trendies passed by on the other side, but a red-faced old boy in a thick scarf stopped and doubled back to drop a couple of euros into her guitar case and nod, 'Good luck, now.'

Towards nightfall a sudden shower scoured the streets of Cork. It drove me along Oliver Plunkett Street and up the steps into the Hi-B. Now that is a bar made in heaven, a warm paradise in ancient plush, firelight and recondite talk. Sartre? Never had any time for the man. Christy Ring, you said? Now there was a nice hurler if you like. Existential, if you like. I saw them goals of his in the '56 Munster final, didn't I, Tommy? Wait till I tell you . . .

NORTH CATHEDRAL

SHANDON
CRAFT CENTRE

ST. ANNE'S CHURCH
('THE BELLS OF
SHANDON')

CORK
CITY

Shandon Street

John Redmond Street

CORK
BUTTER
MUSEUM

FIRKIN
CRANE
INSTITUTE
FOR DANCE

FATHER PROUT

Pope's Quay

Griffith
Bridge

NORTH CHANNEL, RIVER LEE

Camden Quay

Kyrl's Quay

Coal Quay

CORK
OPERA
HOUSE

Christy
Ring
Bridge

Lavitt's Quay

ENGLISH
MARKET

CRAWFORD
ART
GALLERY

Emmet Pl.

HUGUENOT
QUARTER

Paul St.

RORY
GALLAGHER
PLACE

Frenchchurch St.

Carey's Lane

St. Patrick Street

Winter St.

WEST FRONT
OF CATHEDRAL

ENGLISH

MARKET

HI-B BAR

BEAMISH
IRISH STOUT

Princes St.

Plunkett St.

The Hi-B Bar

Grand Parade

Tuckey St.

Oliver
Plunkett St.

TOURIST HOUSE
INFO. CENTRE
(START OF WALK)

Mall

SOUTH

CHANNEL,

BEAMISH &
CRAWFORD
BREWERY

South Main St.

AN
SPAILPÍN
FÁNACH
PUB

South

RIVER

South Gate
Bridge

Nano Nagle
Bridge

LEE

Proby's Quay

Sullivan's
Quay

ST. FIN BARRE'S
CATHEDRAL

VIEW TO
ST. FIN BARRE'S
FROM RIVER LEE,
SOUTH CHANNEL

WAY TO GO

CITY MAP: From Tourist Office (see below).

TRAVEL:

Rail (www.irishrail.ie), bus (www.buseireann.ie) to Cork.

Road: N25, or ferry (http:WWW.FASTNETLINE.COM) from Swansea to Cork.

WALK DIRECTIONS: From TIC, Grand Parade, across Nano Nagle footbridge Sullivan's Quay, Proby's Quay to St Fin Barre's Cathedral. Proby's Quay, across South Gate Bridge, South Main Street, Tuckey Street, Grand Parade to English Market.

From Princes Street exit – St Patrick Street, Carey's Lane into Huguenot Quarter Rory Gallagher Place, Paul Street, Emmet Place, across Christy Ring Bridge, Pope' Quay, John Redmond Street to Cork Butter Museum, Shandon Craft Centre, S Anne's Tower (the 'Bells of Shandon'), North Cathedral.

Leaving Cathedral, right along street; then Shandon Street, across Griffith Bridge Kyrl's Quay, Coal Quay; right at south end of Christy Ring Bridge. Emmet Place, Pau Street, Frenchchurch Street, St Patrick Street, Wintrop Street to Oliver Plunkett Stree (Hi-B bar on corner). Oliver Plunkett Street, Princes Street, South Mall to TIC.

LENGTH: Half-day

GRADE: Easy

DON'T MISS:
- English Market
- Crawford Art Gallery
- Bells of Shandon

REFRESHMENTS: Lunch/breakfast – English Market; lunch/tea – Crawford Ar Gallery café (021-427-4415); drink – An Spailpín Fánach, Hi-B bar.

INFORMATION:

Cork Tourist Office: Grand Parade; 021-425-5100; www.discoverireland.ie/southwest

7

CANON SHEEHAN LOOP, BALLYHOURA MOUNTAINS, CO LIMERICK AND CO CORK

'GLENANAAR, THE GLEN OF slaughter, is a deep ravine, running directly north and south through a lower spur of the mountains that divide Cork and Limerick.' So wrote Canon Patrick Augustine Sheehan in his novel *Glenanaar*, published in 1905 when the Mallow-born author had been ten years the parish priest of Doneraile. Canon Sheehan might be largely overlooked these days, but his name and fame still resonate around Doneraile and in the Ballyhoura Mountains whose landscape and people he depicted with humour and humanity in a long string of books.

What Ballyhoura is celebrated for these days is walking. Ballyhoura International Walking Festival is one of the showpieces of Irish walking, and the Ballyhoura Bears walking club has a well-earned reputation for combining hiking and *craic* to delectable effect. It was Cal McCarthy, a dedicated Bear and knowledgeable Patrick Sheehan fan, who volunteered to show us around the Canon Sheehan Loop, a superb walk through Glenanaar Forest in the southern ranges of Ballyhoura.

Walking the forest track, we gazed south over 'Canon Sheehan Country'. The vale around Doneraile and Kildorrery lay low, its frosted hills riding like islands in a smoky sea of mist. Canon Sheehan brought out just this wintry aspect in *Glenanaar*: 'As the weather was intensely cold, there were none of the usual thaws, but the frost knit the snow-flakes together and crusted them all over with its own hard but brilliant enamelling. The white level plain stretched its monotone of silver till it touched the sky-line, and was merged in it.'

The outstretched hand of Cal indicated the line of an ancient trackway, an icy streak of silver making like an arrow for the distant Nagle Mountains. 'An Claidh Dubh, the Black Ditch,' said our guide. 'It's been traced a long way. Iron Age, perhaps? A boundary, but between who or what?' He smiled. 'There's just so much we don't know about what's in our land – which just feeds the old curiosity!'

We turned across the hill and came to a mossy old Mass Rock, three-sided and massive, lying under the trees. Rumours of a priest shot while praying here, tales of his burial under a pile of stones on the banks of the Ogeen River. Down there we encountered ancient broadleaved trees bearded and coiffed with frozen mosses, unearthly snow formations like arctic candyfloss, and the cold exhalations of the Ogeen as it rushed over its sandstone bed.

Patrick Sheehan was a quiet man, by all accounts, but he wasn't afraid to promulgate land reform, education, political freedom and inter-faith co-operation. Through his eyes we see the old Irish countrymen 'in their strong frieze cutaway coats, their drab or snuff-coloured vests and knee-breeches, the rough home-woven stockings, and the strong shoes – all made, like themselves, for hard work and wild tempestuous weather.' Sheehan lamented in *Glenanaar*: 'No Wordsworth has yet sung the praises of these Irish dalesmen.' He himself did the job – superbly, too.

As we crossed the Ogeen River and came up the ice-puddled track, we puzzled over the slaughter that gave Glenanaar its ominous name. Bard Ossian tells of a great battle between Clann Morna and Clann Baskin at the Ford of Light on the Ounnageeragh or Ogeen River. Was it that ancient blood-letting? Then what of 'The Battle of the Raven's Glen', the ballad that describes O'Sullivan Beare ambushing a force of 'Saxons and kerns from the wilds of Duhallow' on the same spot?

Then O'Sullivan burst like the angel of slaughter,
On the foe by the current of Geeragh's wild water,
And his brave men of Cork and of Kerry's wild regions
Were the rushing destroyers, his death-dealing legions;
And onward they rode over traitor and craven,
Whose bones long bestrewed the lone Glen of the Raven.

That's as close as we're likely to get to what actually happened in Glenanaar – if indeed anything happened at all. You know what storytellers are like.

MASS ROCK

GLENANAAR FOREST

OGEEN or OUNNAGEERAGH RIVER

TOLKIEN TREES WITH WEIRD MOSS BEARDS!

TO ARDPATRICK & KILMALLOCK

CAR PARK (START)

MASS ROCK

AN CLAIDH DUBH

(THE BLACK DITCH)

FROSTED LEAVES

SUPERB VIEWS OVER 'CANON SHEEHAN COUNTRY'!

CANON SHEEHAN LOOP
BALLYHOURA MOUNTAINS
CO. LIMERICK/ CO. CORK

WAY TO GO

MAP: OS of Ireland 1:50,000 Discovery 73; downloadable map/instructions (highly recommended) at www.discoverireland.ie/walking.

TRAVEL:

From Kilmallock, R512 Kildorrery road. 2 km beyond Ardpatrick, right (brown 'Ballyhoura Forest' sign). In 4 miles, 'Ballyhoura-Glenanair' sign points right to forest car park.

WALK DIRECTIONS (Canon Sheehan Loop/CSL – blue arrows): Pass striped pole; down track; cross Ogeen River. *NB This walk follows CSL in reverse!* Ignore CSL arrows to right; keep ahead left, up track to T-junction at top. Left (purple arrow/PA); follow track along hillside. In 1½ miles, where track begins to descend, right (CSL, PA) up rising track. In 100 m, pass Mass Rock (signposted left); continue ½ mile, descending to cross tracks and continue down to cross river. Turn right beside river, soon recrossing to right bank. In ¼ mile, pass 'Mass Rock' fingerpost/CSL on right; in another ¼ mile, at next 'Mass Rock'/CSL/PA, left down bank; path to recross footbridge; track to car park.

LENGTH: 5 miles: allow 2–2½ hours.

GRADE: Moderate

CONDITIONS: Forest tracks.

DON'T MISS:
• fantastic views over 'Canon Sheehan Country'
• the Mass Rock
• Tolkienesque trees by the Ogeen River

REFRESHMENTS: None en route – take a picnic.

INFORMATION:

Ballyhoura Fáilte Tourist Information Office: Kilfinane, Co Limerick; 063-91300; www.ballyhouracountry.com.

8

DOLMEN LOOP, LISVERNANE, GLEN OF AHERLOW, CO TIPPERARY

IF YOU WANT TO meet a man with a twinkle in his eye, go walking with Michael Moroney of Lisvernane in County Tipperary. I've rarely seen so much enthusiasm for a well-loved landscape, so much energy and good humour packed into one human frame.

Which of the many Glen of Aherlow walking routes to follow, that was the question. 'The Dolmen Loop up Slievenamuck,' proposed Michael. 'We'll get a view of the Galtees from up there that'll make you glad you went.'

Slievenamuck is a beautiful hill, a smooth climb to an outstanding view. We set off four strong from Moroney's pub in Lisvernane – Michael, Jane and myself, along with County Tipperary poet and mountain rescue man Jimmy Barry. Up the muddy boreens behind Lisvernane we trudged, getting well mud-bespattered for our trouble, following the reassuring red arrows of the Dolmen Loop as they led us through the trees and up the open spine of Slievenamuck.

At the top of the mountain we found the lichen-blotched grey structure of Shrough dolmen, a massive portal tomb built to hold the mortal remains of Stone Age grandees some 5,000 years ago. No one with an ounce of soul could fail to appreciate just why this spot was chosen at the crest of a hill commanding such a view as this, the whole uplift of the Galtees spread superbly under a muted sky, their high tops and flanks still streaked with late snowfall, seen in full glory across the glen that opened 1,000 feet below. And how could such a resting place fail to be one of the beds of that amorous fugitive pair, Diarmuid and Gráinne?

'Cush there on the left,' said Michael, pointing out the peaks, 'with Greenane behind; then Galtybeg rising to Galtymore, where you were last summer with Jimmy.' White strings of snow ran down the gullies in the face of Galtymore. The strings of a blind harper, declared Jimmy, a bit of a chancer who had tried to entice the ladies of Slievenamon over to the Galtees with his music. We gazed west to where Slievenamon lay 25 miles away, a curvaceous grey-blue mountain curled on a bed of mist like a Henry Moore sculpture of a reclining woman.

There was definitely something in the air of Slievenamuck today. Michael put his head back and sent 'Sweet Aherlow' floating over his native glen. I groaned out 'The Flower of Magherally'. Jane wisely kept her counsel. And Jimmy gave us chapter and verse of 'The Exile's Return':

> Old scenes, old songs, old friends again,
> The vale and the cot I was born in—
> O, Ireland, up from my heart of hearts
> I bid you the top o' the mornin'!

Moving on was a wrench. But we had the graceful curl of Slievenamon as a lodestone in front of us, as we headed west along rocky, peaty rides left open by Coillte in the young plantations that now cover the upper flanks of Slievenamuck. Lower down we passed

two giant exotic conifers, 'the tallest trees in the world', Michael averred, '. . . well, they would be if they were let grow tall enough. But they're the tallest trees in Aherlow, anyhow.'

Down in the glen once more, we passed Ballinacourty House, once the seat of the Massey-Dawson family and now

SHROUGH DOLMEN
(DIARMUID &
GRAINNE'S
BED)

STUNNING
PANORAMA
OF GALTEES
FROM HERE

SLIEVENAMON

ABANDONED
BOOTS!

FINE VIEWS
FROM HERE

SLIEVENAMUCK

PART OF PADRAIGH'S LOOP

BENCH

ON SLIEVENAMUCK
WITH SLIEVENAMON
IN THE DISTANCE

MUDDY!

THE AVENUE

BALLINACOURTY
HOUSE

A FINE
RESTAURANT

MORONEY'S PUB
(START & FINISH)

LISVERNANE

JIMMY, CHRISTOPHER,
JANE & MICHAEL OUTSIDE
MORONEY'S
PUB

RIVER AHERLOW

GREAT CRAIC,
GREAT PINT!

TO TIPPERARY
TOWN

GALTYMORE

DOLMEN LOOP,
LISVERNANE
CO. TIPPERARY

GALTEE MOUNTAINS

GALTEES PANORAMA

a top-notch hotel. I followed the others, taking my time, savouring the view of the Galtees and looking forward to a nice pint in Moroney's, the taste of another of Jimmy Barry's poems on my tongue:

> Sliabhnamon,
> This mountain of the women
> is our high stool, with every
> gulp of frosty air we
> get drunk on her beauty.
> This night that will never
> come again . . .

WAY TO GO

MAP: OS of Ireland 1:50,000 Discovery 66, 74; downloadable map/instructions (highly recommended) at www.discoverireland.ie/walking.

TRAVEL:

Rail (www.irishrail.ie): Tipperary (15 miles).

Road: N8 to Cashel, N74 to Tipperary, R664 to Newtown, R663 to Lisvernane.

WALK DIRECTIONS (follow red arrows): From Moroney's pub, left; in 200 m, left (arrows on wall) up lane. In ⅓ mile, right (arrows) up muddy boreen. In 200 m, right (arrows) up forest track. Left at top (arrows). In ¼ mile, Pádraigh's Loop (blue arrows) curves right; but go left here (red arrow, 'Ballyhoura Way' sign), then left again (arrow) down through trees. Right (arrow) up boreen; follow this for ¾ mile to bench. Sharp right (arrow) up ridge of Slievenamuck for 1 mile to dolmen at summit. On for 250 m; right (arrow) through young trees for 150 m; left on lower track. Then follow arrows east for 1 mile, to turn right (arrow) on grassy path going west. In 300 m Pádraigh's Loop rejoins; in another ½ mile hairpin back to left (arrows) down through trees for ½ mile to The Avenue. Right (arrows) for ¾ mile to road junction; right into Lisvernane.

Cont.

LENGTH: 7 miles: allow 3–4 hours.

GRADE: Moderate

CONDITIONS: Muddy on the forest tracks.

DON'T MISS:
- views of the Galtees and Slievenamon from Slievenamuck
- Shrough dolmen a.k.a. Diarmuid and Gráinne's Bed
- a pint in Moroney's after the walk

REFRESHMENTS: Moroney's pub, Lisvernane (062-56156).

INFORMATION:

Glen of Aherlow Walking Festival (May–June and Jan–Feb): www.aherlow.com.

Tourist Office: Cashel Heritage Centre; 062-62511; www.discoverireland.ie.

9

COUMDUALA LOUGH, COMERAGH MOUNTAINS, CO WATERFORD

BREAKFAST AT HANORA'S COTTAGE – now that's a god-like start to a misty day among the Comeragh Mountains. Is there a cosier centre of warmth and cheer in County Waterford? When Mary Wall and her husband Seamus first came to live here in the Nire Valley in 1967, Hanora's Cottage was just that, a little cottage of two rooms hardly altered since it was built for Seamus's great-grandparents. These days Seamus has sadly passed on, and Mary runs the much-extended and modernised house with her son Eoin and his wife Judith. But Hanora's Cottage continues to burnish the lamp of hospitality, just as Seamus would have wished.

It was Michael Hickey who turned up at eight on the dot to take Jane and me walking in the mountains – a man of his hands (some of the beautiful woodwork in Hanora's Cottage is of his crafting), and a man of the hills whom you would trust to take you there and lead you back through all winds and weathers. On the hillside at the end of the valley road we turned round and round, spellbound, as Michael named the peaks and hollows of a stunning panorama for us – westward to the golden Galtees and darkly clouded Knockmealdowns across the border in Tipperary, south to the nearer Tooreen ridge with its component high corries of Coumfea, the Deer Hollow, and Curraghduff, the Black Moor that shelters the twin loughs of Sgilloge.

For 500 million years the wind and rain, frost and sun have been slowly moulding these sandstone conglomerate mountains with their winking white chips of quartz. Michael pointed out standing stones and ancient burial barrows across the hillsides far below, and the talk turned to the long tide-like movements of time, the rise and fall of civilisations and of modes of burial and commemoration. 'The eternal question we go on asking down the years,' mused Michael as he stared over the valley. 'Why do we have to age? Why do we have to leave?'

We followed a sedgy old green road, studded with stones and marked with white posts, eastward towards The Gap, a saddle of ground between Knockanaffrin, the Mass Hill, and Knockaunapeebra, the Little Hill of the Piper. Who was the piper? Michael didn't know; but he did have a great saucy story of Fionn MacCumhaill and the women of Sliabh na mBan, at which we laughed like hyenas as we walked the track among sheep whose red flock-marks had run in the rain to dye their fleeces the campest of pinks.

From The Gap the view east was immense, way across Waterford and Kilkenny into Carlow and Wexford, wave upon wave of steel-blue hills floating in mist and running on towards Mount Leinster and the Blackstairs. 'This is why I come out walking,' said Michael. 'For me it's a necessity. All my days I've *had* to be outside, walking these hills,' and he looked around like a man drawing in the very breath of life.

Turning our backs on this magical prospect at last, we forged steeply uphill over knolls and dips, by crusty outcrops of black rock. Mist began to swirl across, but with a fence as guide we were soon up on the spine of Knockanaffrin, balanced gingerly at the very rim of a scoop of sheer cliffs and looking down on Lough Coumduala lying 500 feet below, pear-shaped, with the muted gleam of a polished bronze mirror. Beyond rose the blue hills, each an island lapped by a river of mist.

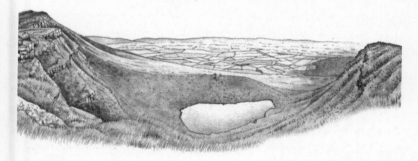

Descending the steep breast of the Mass Hill, Michael Hickey flung out an arm to embrace Comeraghs, Galtees and Knockmealdowns. 'If only people would lift their eyes from working 24 hours a day and look what's there for the taking, they'd all be out walking.'

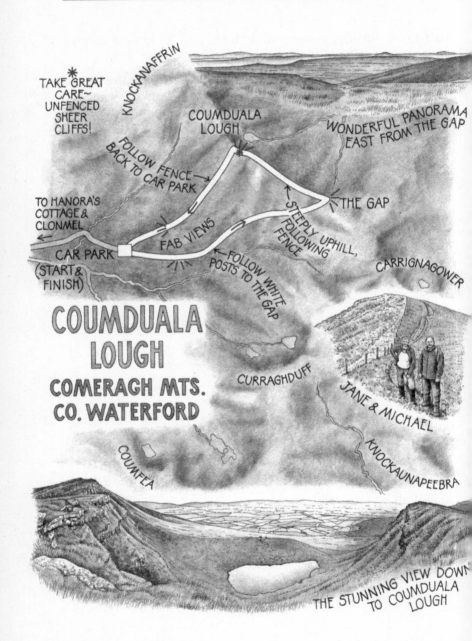

KNOCKANAFFRIN

TAKE GREAT
CARE ~
UNFENCED
SHEER
CLIFFS!

COUMDUALA
LOUGH

WONDERFUL PANORAMA
EAST FROM THE GAP

FOLLOW FENCE
BACK TO CAR PARK

THE GAP

TO HANORA'S
COTTAGE &
CLONMEL

STEEPLY UPHILL,
FOLLOWING
FENCE

CARRIGNAGOWER

FAB VIEWS

CAR PARK
(START &
FINISH)

FOLLOW WHITE
POSTS TO THE GAP

COUMDUALA
LOUGH
COMERAGH MTS.
CO. WATERFORD

CURRAGHDUFF

JANE & MICHAEL

COUMFEA

KNOCKAUNAPEEBRA

THE STUNNING VIEW DOWN
TO COUMDUALA
LOUGH

WAY TO GO

MAP: OS of Ireland 1:50,000 Discovery 75.

TRAVEL:

Rail (www.irishrail.ie): Clonmel (12 miles).

Bus (www.buseireann.ie): 386 (Tuesdays), 388 (Fridays) to Ballymacarbry (4 miles from Hanora's Cottage).

Road: N24 to Clonmel; R671 (Dungarvan road) to Ballymacarbry; left on minor road to pass Hanora's Cottage near Labartt's Bridge; continue for 2 miles to car park at end of road (OS of I ref. S 278128).

WALK DIRECTIONS: From car park, follow brown 'The Gap' sign and white posts uphill, making for a wall on your right. Cross wall through gate; follow white posts for 1½ miles on moorland path to a stile at The Gap. Left here, steeply uphill with a fence on your right. In ¾ mile another fence comes into view, running downhill to left. Cross fence on your right by stile here; go to edge of cliffs to view Coumduala Lough. (*NB Please take great care! Unfenced sheer cliffs!*) Continue along fence for 100 yards to recross by another stile; turn downhill with fence on your left, and follow it back to car park.

LENGTH: 4 miles: allow 2–3 hours.

GRADE: Hard

CONDITIONS: Rough moorland tracks; avoid in heavy mist. Steep upward climb from The Gap to Coumduala Lough viewpoint.

DON'T MISS:
- south and westward views from Knockanaffrin
- eastward views from The Gap
- prospect over Coumduala Lough from the cliffs

REFRESHMENTS: None en route – take a picnic.

INFORMATION:

Tourist Office: Mary Street, Clonmel (052-612-2960; www.discoverireland.ie/south-east).

Guided walks: Contact Hanora's Cottage, Nire Valley, Ballymacarbry, Co Waterford (052-613-6134; www.hanorascottage.com).

10
KILMACOLIVER HILL, CO KILKENNY

THE SPRING WATER CAME gushing out of the roadside wall on the outskirts of Tullaghought, falling with a quiet splash and rustle across Jane's fingers and into its basin. Over the road stood an information board bright with images of butterflies with seductive names – holly blue, small copper, painted lady, red admiral. The pond beyond was skinned with green, its scrub willows loud with wrens and chaffinches. 'Like the lake,' said the noticeboard's quotation from Henry Thoreau's *Walden*, 'my serenity is rippled but not ruffled.' A very apposite notion on a breezy, sunny day down in the south-west marches of Kilkenny.

Eoin Hogan, the county walks officer, had joined us for this morning's ramble, and we made good time along the shaded lanes at the foot of Kilmacoliver Hill. The minuscule black pimples of the ancient stone circle at the summit of the hill pricked the skyline and called us on past buttercup meadows in which the cropping sheep were almost swallowed up in rippling shallows of gold. Two skittish colts were being unloaded from a horsebox in a farm gateway, their hooves clattering as they tittuped backwards down the ramp.

A long mile up the mountain at the ruined farm of Bregaun, all was still. Maidenhair ferns sprang from the naked gables, moss lay thick in the window frames, and sinews of ivy were slowly and silently easing the damp old walls into their component stones. 'Imagine the trek you'd have down to so-called civilisation,' mused Eoin as we stood in the tree shadows, 'and the hunger you'd have to know what was going on down there in the world.'

The path led up through open fields pungent with pineapple-scented mayweed. At the summit of Kilmacoliver Hill a great circle of rough and jagged rocks enclosed the recumbent, weather-eroded stones of a megalithic tomb – a monument simple, massive and solemn. The flatlands of Kilkenny stretched north for maybe 40 miles, the humpy spine of the Comeragh Mountains rose in Waterford far to the south-west, and nearer at hand the Hill of the Women, Sliabhnamon, curled gracefully in a reclining female shape of slate blue and pearly grey. We lingered long over this breathtaking prospect, perching on the sun-warmed stones and basking in the warmth of midday.

Descending the northern slopes of Kilmacoliver Hill, the chat turned to country walking in Ireland and the current nationwide efforts to get it properly off the ground. As always when one's talking of the tangled and painstaking business of setting up viable, legally sited walks in rural Ireland, lots of pies feel the presence of a good many fingers. The European Union's LEADER programme funds rural development schemes across Europe, provided that they closely involve local people; and, as Eoin told us, Trail Kilkenny couldn't have been established without the support of County Kilkenny LEADER partnership, which also financed the setting up of the Kilmacoliver walk. The same story can be told in many different counties across Ireland, the sort of behind-the-scenes activity that you never even think about when you're walking the Sligo shore, say, or crossing the hills of Fermanagh.

Down on the road once more, we stopped to admire a young horse being galloped round a track, hooves pounding, sweat streamers curling off and flying out behind, the red-capped jockey intent in his crouch. Beyond lay a little Gaelic Athletic Association pitch where lush grasses outnumbered players by ten million to nothing. A young girl was carefully painting the wheezy old gate for her daddy. Horse, jockey and girl went about their business in the sunshine, presided over by the green head of Kilmacoliver Hill, at whose crown the old stones stood proud, black and tiny against the blue sky.

CAR PARK (START & FINISH)

TO TULLAGHOUGHT

POND, TREES, SPRING... A BEAUTIFUL SPOT!

SPRING

SHRINE

GAA PITCH

HOUSE WITH WHITE RAILINGS

FARM

TO CARRICK-ON-SUIR

HORSE GALLOPS

PASS BY

GATE

STEP STILE

BREGAUN (RUIN)

KILMACOLIVER HILL

JANE IN THE STONE CIRCLE WITH SLIEVENAMON IN THE BACKGROUND

MEGALITHIC TOMB & STONE CIRCLE

PATH THROUGH FLOWERY FIELDS

FABULOUS VIEWS~ CO. KILKENNY, COMERAGH MTNS & SLIEVENAMON

KILMACOLIVER HILL CO. KILKENNY

PANORAMA FROM KILMACOLIVER HILL WITH SLIEVENAMON

WAY TO GO

MAP: OS of Ireland 1:50,000 Discovery 75; downloadable map/instructions (highly recommended) at www.discoverireland.ie/walking.

TRAVEL:

Rail (www.irishrail.ie) to Carrick-on-Suir (5 miles).

Bus (1890-42-41-41; www.ringalink.ie) to Tullaghought.

Road: From Kilkenny, N76 to Callan; R698, 697 to Tullaghought (signed). Right at village crossroads; trailhead car park in 300 m on right (Loop Walk noticeboard).

WALK DIRECTIONS: Continue along road from car park, passing shrine to Our Lady, then passing side road on right. In 150 m, opposite house with white railings, left up lane (purple arrow waymark/PA). Follow lane round right bend by farm. Track surface turns from tarmac to dirt; continue for nearly 2 km, to go over step stile by gate and pass ruined farmhouse of Bregaun. In 50 m, muddy track swings right into field; but keep ahead here up walled lane (PA) for 70 m, then right up steps to follow PAs through open fields. Keep hedge on left and follow PAs up to triangulation pillar and stone circle on summit of Kilmacoliver Hill. Turn right off hill, following fence line to bottom. Right past gate (don't go over); in 100 m, left over step stile; follow path through woods to road. Left to house with white railings; right to car park.

LENGTH: 4 miles: allow 2 hours.

GRADE: Moderate

DON'T MISS:

- spring and ponds at start of walk
- stone circle and tomb on Kilmacoliver Hill
- view from the hill

REFRESHMENTS: None en route – take a picnic.

INFORMATION:

Walks and activities: www.trailkilkenny.ie.

Kilkenny Tourist Office: 056-775-1500; www.discoverireland.ie/southeast.

11

Carne to Rosslare Harbour, Co Wexford

A GLORIOUS WINTER'S MORNING on Carne jetty, with a peerless blue sky plastered over County Wexford. There was an acrylic intensity to the yellow oilskins of the fishermen and the scarlet paint of the little boats they were busy loading with the day's creels. The sea wind was cold all right, but it blew straight in from the south, with the promise of shoving us along. The strong winter sun, low in the south, lay behind us too, lighting up the cliffs and bellying coastline ahead, elongating our shadows into a pair of flat-out giants that tugged our feet north up the strand.

What a pleasure to be out of the city and down at the shore on such a day It seemed incredible that in County Sligo, only a few short weeks ago, we had been half drowned and frozen on the wettest of walks out at the Low Rosses. Now we ran like a pair of fools until we'd driven all the breath out of us; then sauntered arm in arm on the sands, letting the great curve of the beach draw the eye on along the low sandy cliffs to vanishing point a couple of miles ahead.

It's a sandy scene hereabouts; but under the soft demerara granules lie some of the oldest rocks in the land. Out at sea the dark upturned hull of the Whilkeen Rock broke the small waves into foam, and on the strand lay ancient boulders of granite, hulking and sea-smoothed, criss-crossed with thick raised seams like the back of a much-flogged old salt. The sea had performed its usual casual artistry on that morning's falling tide, strewing the beach with ribbon weeds of shocking pink and lurid green, colours that seemed better suited to some tropical jungle than a cold shore in winter-bound Ireland.

A pair of beach anglers sat stolidly, using their bait boxes as makeshift fishing stools, watching the tips of their sea rods in hopes of a bite. From what? 'Bass, if we're lucky,' they confirmed. 'Beautiful eating, if you can get 'em. Maybe a mackerel or two. Maybe some flatfish.' Brave words, but the catch bag lay empty as yet. There was an even braver man on the sand cliffs near St Helen's, stripped naked to the waist in the wind and facing the ocean in deep absorption. The prospect was all in shades of blue, from the shot silk and jade of the sea through the smoky blue of the horizon to the hard enamel of the cloudless sky.

The path led over the cliffs. Two donkeys came to the fence, one grey and one black, and put their noses over the wire for half a biscuit each. They stretched their soft rubbery upper lips to hoover the treat off my palm, then crunched ruminatively, licking the crumbs from their long yellow teeth.

Down by St Helen's pier we found two items bobbing – one red boat by the jetty, and one pied wagtail on a rock. The wagtail proved the opening salvo in a fusillade of bird life. I'd had no idea that the south-east Wexford coast was so brilliant for wintering birds, though I suppose a glance at the map – all those east-facing headlands and beaches as landfalls – should have alerted me. At all events, once we got to Greenore Point the strands came alive with hurrying, stooping, pattering figures: dunlin, down from the Arctic Circle, playing Grandmother's Footsteps with the oncoming tide; fussy little turnstones with short orange legs, scampering and bickering in groups; a flock of sanderlings all taking off at the same split second, twittering, to swoop with white-edged scimitar wings to a stance a few feet further away from the advancing humans. Just to contemplate the journeys these birds had accomplished to be here made the head spin.

Nondescript, blackish rocks lay in the sea off Greenore Point, drying posts for cormorants with out-held wings. These rocks were ancient when Noah was a lad. They have been lying here for 1,700,000,000 years. That was something to picture as we turned the corner of the headland and made for Rosslare Harbour over a crunchy carpet of clean-picked crab and mussel shells.

ROSSLARE HARBOUR

FERRY TERMINAL

CAR PARK (FINISH)

KILRANE

ALTERNATIVE ROUTE

FOR HIGH TIDE OR BAD WEATHER

LOOK FOR SHORE WADERS ~
DUNLIN, TURNSTONE, SANDERLING

GREENORE POINT
1,700,000,000-
YEAR-OLD
ROCKS!

ST. HELEN'S

ST. HELEN'S PIER

CHURCH

BEAUTIFUL STRANDS!

CARNE TO
ROSSLARE HARBOUR
CO. WEXFORD

WHILKEEN ROCK

CARNE PIER (START)

LIGHTHOUSE INN

CARNE

ON CARNE BEACH

WAY TO GO

MAP: OS of Ireland 1:50,000 Discovery 77; detailed map/instructions in *Slí Charman* booklet guide (see below).

TRAVEL:

Rail (www.irishrail.ie) or bus (www.buseireann.ie) to Rosslare Europort; bus service 378, Wexford–Carne; taxi (087-236-6756 or 087-991-0233) to Carne. Road: N25 towards Rosslare Harbour; at Kilrane, right on minor roads to Carne.

WALK DIRECTIONS: From Carne Pier, walk north along coast to Rosslare Harbour – it's that simple!

NB It's best to do this walk on a falling tide. High tide can make St Helen's Pier and Greenore Point impassable, but you can detour inland from St Helen's to Rosslare Harbour (see map).

LENGTH: 5 miles: allow 2–3 hours.

GRADE: Easy

CONDITIONS: Sandy strands or coast path.

DON'T MISS:
- multicoloured ribbon weed and shells along the strands
- shore waders around Greenore Point
- ancient rocks off Greenore Point – they are 1,700,000,000 years old!

REFRESHMENTS: Lighthouse Inn, Carne (053-913-1131; please ring to check opening times).

INFORMATION:

Tourist Office: Kilrane, near Rosslare Harbour (053-916-1155; www.wexfordtourism.com); www.discoverireland.ie/southeast.

Slí Charman booklet guide by Ray McGrath (County Wexford Partnership), available locally and at TIC.

12

SLIEVEBAWN AND TOMDUFF HILL, BLACKSTAIRS MOUNTAINS, CO CARLOW

T HE CLERK OF THE weather was brewing some ominous stuff up there over the Blackstairs Mountains. What he had up his sleeve for Wexford, though, never quite made it to the Carlow side of the county border. So Jane and I had the rare smug satisfaction of watching all those rain towers toppling on someone else, while ourselves escaping with only a sprinkling. As Brian Gilsenan, the wry Monaghan-born walker who came over the misty hills with us, observed at the summit of Slievebawn: 'If it isn't raining somewhere in view, then you aren't on the Blackstairs.'

The OS map can be deceptive if you don't count your contours right. Looking at all those brown squiggles packed tight together like elvers in a sieve, I'd anticipated quite a pull up from the Nine Stones car park. But in fact the climb to the cairn on Slievebawn is no more than a steady-breathing doddle. The view is the only breathtaking aspect of the ascent: a fantastic stretch north-west across the chequerboard lowlands of Carlow and Kilkenny, cradled between the slopes of Slievebawn and Croaghaun.

Up at the peak we climbed on to the huge boulder of dully glimmering white quartz that marks the summit of Slievebawn. Far below the Nine Stones stood in line abreast. These stumpy standing stones were set up facing that incomparable view as a memorial to a group of shepherds who died after becoming lost in the mist on the Blackstairs. Or maybe, as a more sinister story insists, they are nine sheep herders turned to stone by St Kevin of Glendalough because they refused to share their picnic with him. Kevin was rather prone to rash and vengeful acts, by all accounts, so that version might have a pinch of truth to it. Don't be mean, seemed to be the only moral extricable from the fable.

We hastened to share round the sweeties, and headed south-west along the ridge path. Here was the place to take in the noble aspect of the whole Blackstairs ridge, rising in a series of gradually diminishing undulations on our left hand. This is one of the classic mountain panoramas of Ireland, only truly appreciable from the viewpoint we had gained, the spine of Slievebawn that sticks out a little way to the side of the main range.

The prospect began in the north with the tallest and most dramatic of the Blackstairs Mountains, the great 795-metre pyramid of Mount Leinster, crouching today under mist like the head of an old woman hunched in a lacy shawl. From there the ridge swooped south over Knockroe, dropping to the saddle of the Gap of Scullogue before climbing over Blackstairs Mountain and descending once more towards the twin tumps of Carrigalachan and Carrigroe. 'Caher Roe's Den,' said Brian, pointing out a wilderness of rocky outcrops below Blackstairs Mountain. 'Now he would have been an O'Dempsey, a Laois man, a robber who had his hideout among the rocks. Difficult to winkle him out of there, I'd say.'

It was not only Mount Leinster that stood cowled today. The south-east wind had driven up an enormous roller of cloud, a 100-foot-high wave that clung all the way along the Blackstairs

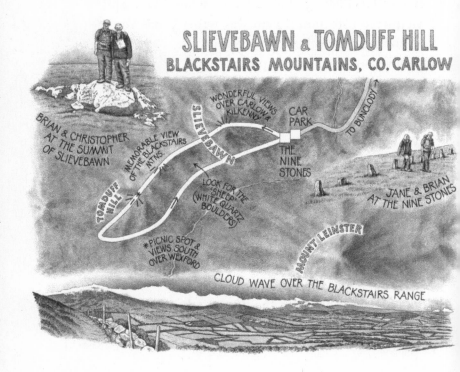

SLIEVEBAWN & TOMDUFF HILL
BLACKSTAIRS MOUNTAINS, CO. CARLOW

ridge, backgrounded by a threatening sky the colour of unpolished slate. It was one of those sights you don't forget, however many more impressive hills or mightier mountains you might have climbed.

The sides of Slievebawn were scattered with quartz boulders, like so many white sheep grazing in the heather. All of a sudden there were real animals on the hill – a herd of horses, maybe a dozen, moving along the summit, as unheralded as if they'd been dropped from the sky. At the end of the ridge we halted on Tomduff Hill to catch the southward view over the stormy plains of Wexford, and then started our homeward circle along the lower edge of the mountain. A sharp shower went slanting across, the orchids in the grass sparkled with raindrops, and the horses faded behind the rain curtain as if they had never been there at all.

———◆•◆•◆———

WAY TO GO

MAP: OS of Ireland 1:50,000 Discovery 68.

TRAVEL:

N80 from Enniscorthy towards Carlow; leaving Bunclody, left on minor road (OSI ref S 908569; brown 'Mount Leinster' sign). In 5 miles, left (835567; 'Nine Stones and TV Transmitter' brown sign) to parking place at top of road (817546).

WALK DIRECTIONS: From car park, turn your back on Mount Leinster and walk up Slievebawn to summit cairn (806548). Then follow ridge for 1 mile to Tomduff Hill (792536); continue downhill, to bear left along wall/fence. Soon it turns uphill; in 400 m, bear right through wall and continue with fence on your right to meet road (801540). Return to Nine Stones car park along road, or along mountainside.

LENGTH: 5 miles: allow 2–3 hours.

GRADE: Moderate

CONDITIONS: Mountain paths, one easy/moderate climb.

DON'T MISS:
- the Nine Stones
- stunning views from ridge path
- lark song that always seems to be present

REFRESHMENTS: Take a picnic – Tomduff Hill is a wonderful spot.

INFORMATION:

Tourist Office: Tullow Street, Carlow (059-91-31554; www.carlowtourism.com).

Guided walks: Contact Brian Gilsenan (053-937-7828 or 086-838-6460; www.moss-cottageireland.com).

13
KYLE LOOP, TINAHELY, CO WICKLOW

I T WAS SHAPING UP to be a lazy afternoon round Tinahely in the hills of South Wicklow. 'Up and on, then,' cried Hugh Coogan, farmer and walker, brandishing his hiking staff. 'Time to work it all off, eh!'

In the jovial company of Hugh and his friend and neighbour Mary O'Connor, Jane and I swung with a will along the Wicklow Way. The first item we passed was a melancholy one, the memorial cross that marks the spot where poor Dr James McNamara shot himself by accident back in 1916 – he was crossing a ditch when his gun snagged against the wire fence and went off. Down the track apiece we came to the seven-gated Ballybeg Rath. Peering inside an ancient hollow ash, I saw a great lump of red and white quartzite gripped deep, as if being swallowed by the leathery old throat of the tree. There was sky-blue brooklime in the stream at Ballycumber Ford, and rain-pearled grass half hiding the marble memorial just up the lane that told the birds and cattle and occasional passing human of the fame of Luke O'Toole, 1873–1929, 'first full-time secretary of the GAA.'

At The Green, Hugh stood contemplating the old schoolhouse on the crossroads. 'All Kyle, all

Carrigroe, all Ballybeg got educated here. My daddy went here.'
Now the old school is a holiday home, and Carrigroe and
Ballybeg get more sophisticated schooling much further afield.
In the lane where the kids once pelted home downhill we swung
our sticks, looking forward to tea at Hugh's home farm of Kyle
just round the curve of the hill.

What visitor to Kyle Farmhouse would be so foolish as to
leave Margaret Coogan's teapot unpunished and her home
baking unscathed? When we stepped out again into the strong
afternoon sunlight, we felt like well-fed monarchs.

I climbed Ballycumber Hill with my back to the view, just
for the pleasure of embracing it at the top. A sublime prospect,
one that those who stick to the famous beauty spots and
summits of Wicklow never see – Eagle Hill with its warty lump
of rock, the wide farming plains of Carlow out west where great
flats of milky rain went sliding across fields, woods and
boglands, and Lugnaquilla's purple back rising like a fish on
the long wave of the northern skyline. 'In Wicklow we can pick
out Lug all the time,' Hugh observed, 'and we scarcely bother
learning the names of the rest.'

South Wicklow holds a more subtle appeal for a walker than
the glamour and drama of the mountainous northern half of
the county. Now dedicated local folk like Hugh, Margaret and
Mary O'Connor, walkers and organisers, doers
and persuaders who really know their
own patch, have turned their
neighbourhood village of Tinahely into
a hub from which walkers can explore
hidden country of enormous, if
understated, charm.

The wind rushed with a sea-like susurration in the young spruce and fir along the crest of Ballycumber Hill as we walked its squelchy path south to another tremendous viewpoint, down over Carlow and Wexford. On the south-west horizon the two counties rose together into the peak of Mount Leinster, capping the Blackstairs range 20 miles off. It was a view to add relish to any *al fresco* snack. Sitting in the heather we whaled into the last of the baking, then bowled down an old green cart track to find the Wicklow Way curling at the foot of the hill once more.

KYLE LOOP, TINAHELY
CO. WICKLOW

TO MOYNE

WICKLOW WAY

KYLE FARMHOUSE

SANDYFORD BRIDGE

ROS AOIBINN (LEFT HERE)

STUNNING VIEWS NORTH TO WICKLOW HILLS & LUGNAQUILLA

MARY, MARGARET & HUGH

CARRIGROE

OLD SCHOOL HOUSE

BALLYCUMBER FORD

BALLYCUMBER HILL

LUKE O'TOOLE'S MEMORIAL

CHRISTOPHER COOLS HIS FEET IN THE FORD

VIEWS WEST INTO CO. CARLOW

BEAR RIGHT OVER STILE

BALLYBEG RATH

LOOK FOR THE ASH TREE THAT SWALLOWED THE QUARTZ STONE!

PANORAMA SOUTH TO MT. LEINSTER & BLACKSTAIRS MTNS. & A GREAT PICNIC SPOT

BALLYBEG

WICKLOW WAY

START

DR. McNAMARA'S MEMORIAL

TINAHELY

TO AUGHRIM R747

PANORAMA OVER KYLE FARM TOWARDS WICKLOW HILLS

WAY TO GO

MAP: OS of Ireland 1:50,000 Discovery 62.

TRAVEL:

M11/N11 to Exit 20; R747 Arklow–Aughrim–Tinahely. Entering village, where road turns sharp left to cross bridge, turn *right* up minor road. Take first left (Mangan's Lane); follow it uphill for a mile to Trailhead at Mangan's (OSI ref T 042748).

WALK DIRECTIONS (Purple arrows/PA; yellow Wicklow Way/WW waymarks):

From Trailhead, follow PA to path junction; right along Wicklow Way (WW) past McNamara Memorial (043751) and Ballybeg Rath (050763) to Ballycumber Ford. Left up surfaced road for ½ mile to pass old school house (044773). Following PA, continue for ½ mile; at right bend (045780), left over stile, up forest track for 300 m, then right on forest road for nearly a mile to road at Sandyford Bridge.

Ahead for ½ mile ('Kyle Farmhouse'). At Ros Aoibinn house gate, left up laneway. Cross Kyle Farmhouse drive; ahead up walled lane. In 50 m, right through gate; follow track uphill, then beside forestry fence along hilltop for 1½ miles. Where fence turns left (029762), follow it left downhill for 350 m; right over stile; follow path opposite downhill through heather to meet cart track. Left to meet Wicklow Way, and return to Trailhead.

LENGTH: 8 miles/14 km: allow 3–4 hours.

GRADE: Moderate

CONDITIONS: Field and forest paths, green lanes, minor roads.

DON'T MISS:

- sensational views from Ballycumber Hill
- Ballybeg Rath
- Luke O'Toole's memorial

REFRESHMENTS: None en route – take a picnic.

INFORMATION:

Bray Tourist Office: The Old Courthouse, Main Street; 01-286-7128; www.visitwicklow.ie.

Tinahely Walking Club: Margaret Coogan, Kyle Farm; 087-285-2997

14

GLENDALOUGH AND GLENEALO, CO WICKLOW

THE RAIN-ENGORGED GLENEALO AND Glendasan Rivers were smashing their whitened heads together as they ran into one another in full fury. Standing on the footbridge below the monastic site at the mouth of Glendalough, Jane and I watched the struggle and heard the deep rumble of riverbed stones on the move.

The tall stone finger of the monastery's Round Tower and the dark walls of its ancient churches rose beyond the confluence. The monks who built the 100-foot-high round tower inserted a doorway three times the height of a man above the ground. An entrance far above the spear points of potential attackers, reached by a retractable ladder, was a necessity in the wild Dark Ages era when the tower was constructed – an era when marauding Vikings would burn a monastery and slaughter its monks as a matter of course. They did it to 'Glendalough the Golden' more than once.

When St Kevin first came to Glendalough early in the 6th century AD there was no whiff of monastic glory about the place. The uninhabited 'Valley of the Two Lakes', shadowy and ill-omened with dark crags hemming in two steel-black lakes, must have seemed the most forbidding place in the Kingdom of Leinster. That was precisely its appeal to Kevin, a fiercely ascetic, independent-minded and determined hermit of the most extreme rigour.

We followed the old pilgrim track called the Green Road along the south shore of the Lower Lake, a sheet of gunmetal in which the mountain slopes were hazily reflected. The sombre beauty of Glendalough slowly unfurled itself as the narrow valley swung to the right and revealed a perfect swoop of crags and mountain tops ahead. Tits and goldfinches were squeaking and flirting in the valley bottom trees, but it was the dark silhouette of a big bird of prey, circling smoothly against the hurrying clouds, that held my gaze.

Poulanass Waterfall was a mighty succession of water sluices today, hurling itself down gleaming black chutes of rock. In the forest above, every heather sprig and spruce needle held a drop of yesterday's rain. Our boots skidded and slipped on the railway sleeper steps as we climbed to the viewpoint at the very edge of the Spinc crags, head-spinningly high over Glendalough.

From here, 1,000 feet above the valley floor, the Lower Lake seemed a ragged-edged pewter disc embedded in dark trees. Opposite, outcrops of mica schist in the cliffs of the valley flank rippled like flesh. As we walked on along the boardwalk the Upper Lake appeared, a broad bar of indigo whose western end lay scarred with pale mounds of quartz spoil left by 19th-century lead miners and smelters. The blue-lipped, emphysemic labourers of the Upper Lake, forgotten in their wilderness, lived as hard and unregarded as any hermit saint.

Once over the crest of the Spinc the boardwalk began a

gentle descent that ended above the brawling water of the Glenealo River in the hanging valley beyond the Upper Lake. The river raced through this bleakly beautiful upland to tumble 500 feet into Glendalough in rainy spate. We got across by the footbridge, then skeltered down the zigzag track cut by the miners to reach their levels in the upper glen. The old smelting mill lay in ruins at the foot of the falls, where we sloshed through several rivulets to gain the path back down through the valley.

Glancing across the Upper Lake as we walked the homeward track, we made out the black mouth of St Kevin's Bed, a tiny cave precariously high in a north-facing rock face where the self-denying hermit would watch and pray. The gloomy niche lies permanently in shadow all through the long months of winter. But this evening it looked out on a view of water and hill slopes illuminated by late sunshine from the south and west, gloriously lighting lake, forest and mountainside.

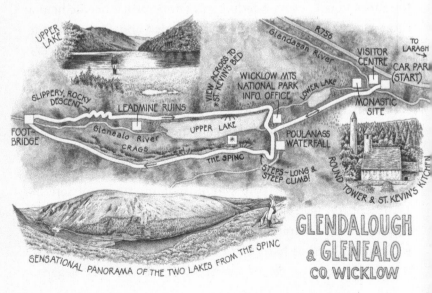

SENSATIONAL PANORAMA OF THE TWO LAKES FROM THE SPINC

GLENDALOUGH & GLENEALO CO. WICKLOW

Way to go

MAPS: OS of Ireland 1:50,000 Discovery 56, or 1:25,000 Glendalough & Glenmalure (widely available locally); Glendalough site and trails map (from Wicklow Mountains National Park Information Office, Upper Lake car park); downloadable map/instructions (highly recommended) at www.discoverireland.ie/walking.

TRAVEL:

Bus (www.glendaloughbus.com): St Kevin's Bus daily from Dublin.

Road: From Dublin – M50 Jct 12; R115 to Laragh; right to car park at Glendalough Visitor Centre.

WALK DIRECTIONS: From Visitor Centre, follow yellow 'walking man'/WM waymarks across river; turn right ('Green Road to Upper Lake') past monastery, to Wicklow Mountains National Park Information Office between lakes. 50 yards past office, left over stream ('Poulanass Waterfall'). Follow yellow arrows up by Poulanass fall, and on up Wicklow Way. Where it turns left across river, bear right (white arrow/WA). On 2nd bend, right (WA), up steep stepped path through trees. At top follow WA along Spinc cliffs and into Glenealo. Cross footbridge; right; steep rocky path down to Upper Lake; follow paths back to car park.

LENGTH: 8½ miles: allow 4 hours.

GRADE: Hard

BUGGY-FRIENDLY: Lakeside paths.

CONDITIONS: Very steep ascent to cliff path; steep rocky descent to Upper Lake.

DON'T MISS:
- Glendalough Monastery
- view down lakes from Spinc cliffs
- St Kevin's Bed

REFRESHMENTS: Plenty around Glendalough; picnic on Spinc cliffs.

INFORMATION:

Glendalough Visitor Centre: 0404-45352; www.glendalough.ie.

15

BRAY TO GREYSTONES, CO WICKLOW

'When the train whistles in and it takes me away
you know I won't look back at all . . .'

WHOEVER CHOSE EAMONN BONNER'S 'Climbing Out of the Window' as the Poet's Corner display in my DART carriage chose well and wisely. Rattling out of Dublin on the way to Bray, looking forward to shaking the winter grime of the city from my psychological shoes, the poem's railway-flavoured themes of regret-free leaving and renewal chimed exactly with my mood. I said as much to Jane, but she was more intent on what was outside the window – black-backed gulls crammed on to the long tongue of Booterstown sandspit, a kingfisher-blue sky over distant Howth, and a dolphin's fin making a brief dark cut in the heavy viscous silk of Killiney Bay.

Bray Harbour yielded one of those instantly vanishing seen-from-a-train cameos: an old man feeding a score of swans and a cloud of herring gulls with fragments of biscuit from a paper bag. We disembarked at Bray  station with its bright commemorative murals, and went out and down to the windy seafront. The house at the seaward end of Martello Terrace where James Joyce lived as a boy stood modestly by the sea, with the sound of the waves slapping up against the harbour steps. Along the promenade couples strolled arm in arm. The sea grumbled and growled against the shingle, and a shaft of sun moved a gold bar across the dark lump of Bray Head.

Up on the cliff path it was sheer blowy magic. The walkway snaked back and forth, clinging dramatically to the face of the cliffs, with breathtaking views over the low wall down to a succession of tunnels into which the serpentine green DART trains vanished, to wriggle through the headlands of Bray Head and Cable Rock. The Dublin, Wicklow & Wexford Railway Company knew a good thing and a captive audience when they saw them, and it was they who built both walkway and railway in the 1850s. It was not all plain sailing: after only 20 years of operation the magnificent Brabazon Tunnel at the very edge of the sea had to be abandoned, and another parallel one dug further inland, because of sea erosion and rock falls.

Looking down from our eyrie on the trains and the tunnels was one species of thrill; another was the wide and beautiful prospect of coast and sea from hunched Howth and tree-smothered Killiney Hill to the steepling rock strata of the cliffs at our elbows, then on south to where the construction cranes were endlessly dipping and swinging over Greystones Harbour. 'All I can say,' murmured a man we met, as he frowned down at the vast development, 'is that we should enjoy the places we've loved all our lives while we can still recognise them.'

Winter storms had crumbled the low clay cliffs near Greystones, forcing us and the path inland. Jane walked ahead in her scarlet balaclava. From Little Red Riding Hood it was a short jump to Beauty and the Beast – namely, a ginger puss curled on a windowsill, lapping up the sunshine, while a huge Alsatian howled mournfully in the living room on the other side of the glass. As the hound watched through the window like a disconsolate lover, the cat got up, stretched with elastic self-satisfaction, leaped lightly down, and led us off towards Greystones and the DART. It must have been reading Bonner, because I'm damned if I didn't hear it purring:

> 'I've just climbed out of my window
> I've just stepped out of my mind
> and I'm catching the last train at midnight and leaving
> my old life behind.'

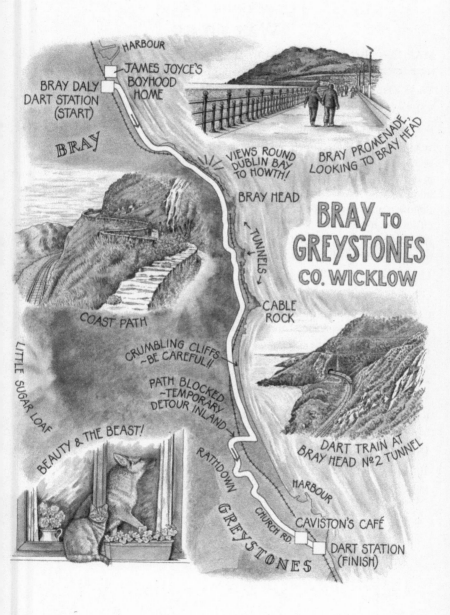

HARBOUR

JAMES JOYCE'S
BOYHOOD
HOME

BRAY DALY
DART STATION
(START)

BRAY

VIEWS ROUND
DUBLIN BAY
TO HOWTH!

BRAY PROMENADE,
LOOKING TO BRAY HEAD

BRAY HEAD

BRAY TO
GREYSTONES
CO. WICKLOW

TUNNELS

CABLE
ROCK

COAST PATH

CRUMBLING CLIFFS
~BE CAREFUL!!

PATH BLOCKED
~TEMPORARY
DETOUR INLAND→

DART TRAIN AT
BRAY HEAD Nº 2 TUNNEL

LITTLE SUGAR LOAF

BEAUTY & THE BEAST!

RATHDOWN

GREYSTONES

HARBOUR

CHURCH RD.

CAVISTON'S CAFÉ

DART STATION
(FINISH)

WAY TO GO

MAP: OS of Ireland 1:50,000 Discovery 56; downloadable map/instructions (highly recommended) at www.discoverireland.ie/walking.

TRAVEL:

Rail (www.irishrail.ie): DART to Bray; return from Greystones.

Bus: 84 or 184 (www.dublinbus.ie).

WALK DIRECTIONS: Left out of Bray Daly station, right over railway, right along seafront promenade, up on to cliffs. Follow cliff path to Greystones DART station. At present Greystones Harbour development blocks path at Rathdown – notices point inland. Cross DART, up lane; opposite 'Rockfort', left into Rathdown housing estate. Follow road round right bend; left after bend; bear right across wide green, down cul-de-sac marked '266-280'. Along laneway on right of yellow house; on along road. At fingerpost '123-147', left between bollards. Follow several right–left doglegs towards sea to reach Centra garage. Forward along Church Road to station.

LENGTH: 6 miles: allow 3 hours.

GRADE: Easy/Moderate

CONDITIONS: NB Cliffs approaching Greystones are crumbling and potentially dangerous – stay well back from edge. Line of path may change owing to landslips.

DON'T MISS:

- view back round Dublin Bay
- disused Brabazon tunnel far below cliff path
- creamy seafood chowder in Caviston's

REFRESHMENTS: Caviston's Café, Church Road, Greystones (01-287-7637) – fabulous food, friendliest service.

INFORMATION:

Tourist Office: Main Street, Bray; 01-286-7128; www.visitwicklow.ie.

Bray Cliffwalk to Greystones leaflet from Bray Tourist Office.

16

PAT LIDDY'S DUBLIN

'*A WEE D'YEH?*' HOARSELY called the paper-seller on Essex Quay. '*A wee d'YEH??*' Jane and I looked enquiringly at our guide and companion Pat Liddy, immaculate in dark overcoat and black fedora – or maybe a trilby, we never quite cleared that up. '*Evening Herald*,' Pat translated. 'That's been shouted on the streets of Dublin ever since I can remember.'

Pat's the man to walk you through the city. You could fit on a pinhead what he doesn't know, or can't spin out of fresh air on the spur of the moment. 'Now here's the Brazen Head – do you know there's been a tavern on this spot for 2,000 years? And speaking of drink, now, we'll cross Father Mathew's Bridge. He was a temperance priest who got 200,000 to sign the pledge. Wonder if he'd have any luck nowadays?'

If any one man outdoes Pat Liddy in Dublinociousness, that would have to be Peter Condell, the crypt guide at St Michan's Church on the Northside. 'We've a journalist here,' murmured Pat, indicating yours truly. 'Fetch the garlic!' snapped Peter. We admired the Baroque musical instruments carved into the case of the venerable organ on whose small keyboard Handel practised in the early 1740s while living in Dublin – no doubt with the tunes from his just-composed *Messiah* rattling around in his psyche. Then

Peter led us outside and into the crypt, making full play of creaking trapdoor, cobwebbed archway and sepulchral commentary, to introduce us to the dusty corpses under St Michan's which are preserved in their wooden coffins by an arcane conjunction of methane, limestone and dry, cool air.

Along Mary's Lane the forklifts beeped as they dashed about the handsome and cavernous Fruit and Vegetable Market, charioteered by beefy, bestubbled men in fluorescent jerkins. Fish and fruit sprang immortalised in red sandstone on the external brackets – flounder, cod, beetroots, leeks. In the playground in nearby Halston Street we took a trip to the Dark Side, hearing of the fearsome gaol that once stood there – 'Newgate Prison,' expounded Pat, 'a hanging prison, a place where patriots were kept before being transported.'

The monument in the centre of the little park carried faded medallions with bas-relief likenesses of the Sheares brothers, fiery John and gentle Henry, barristers, Corkmen and United Irishmen of 1798, betrayed, captured, condemned and executed together on this spot, then buried in the vaults under St Michan's. Just beyond loomed Green Street courthouse, scene of Robert Emmet's speech from the dock – 'When my country takes her place among the nations of the earth, then, and not till then, let my epitaph be written.'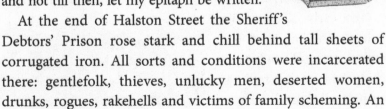

At the end of Halston Street the Sheriff's Debtors' Prison rose stark and chill behind tall sheets of corrugated iron. All sorts and conditions were incarcerated there: gentlefolk, thieves, unlucky men, deserted women, drunks, rogues, rakehells and victims of family scheming. An

1809 police report described a filthy, verminous hell-hole where the sewers didn't function and the bankrupt inmates had to pay the corrupt keeper for their 'accommodation'. One story says the Duke of Wellington did time here as a young man in debt, released only through the generosity (and enlightened self-interest) of his bootmaker.

How to finish our Pat Liddy walk in a sweeter frame of mind? Up in the air on a Ferris wheel in Wolfe Tone Park, contemplating the yarn-spinner's Dublin, and then down to earth in the 18th-century galleried church of St Mary's, better known these days as The Church pub, listening to another 'Wait'll I tell you' from the mighty Liddy, black trilby (or fedora) on the table, while regarding him over a creamy pint. Mmmm-*mmmm!*

WAY TO GO

MAP: Dublin city centre maps from Dublin Tourism Centre, Suffolk St.

TRAVEL:

Luas (www.luas.ie) – Jervis St or Abbey St (Red Line), St Stephen's Green (Green Line); DART (http://www.dublin.ie/transport/dart.htm) – Tara St.

WALK DIRECTIONS: From Dublin Tourism Centre, left along Suffolk St – Dame Lane – Dame Street (**City Hall**). Right down Parliament St; left along Essex Quay (**Isolde's Tower**). Fishamble St – Cook St (**St Audoen's Gate, City Walls**) – Bridge St (**Brazen Head**) – **Fr Mathew Bridge** – Church St (**St Michan's Church**). Right along Mary's Lane (**Fruit & Vegetable Market**) – Halston St (**Newgate Gaol site, Sheare Brothers' monument, Debtor's Prison**) – Green St (**Courthouse**). Mary St (**The Church pub**) – Jervis St – Wolfe Tone Park – Ormond Quay Lower – Wellington Quay – **Temple Bar** – Anglesea St – College Green – Dublin Tourism Centre.

LENGTH: Allow half a day.

GRADE: Easy

DON'T MISS:

- Isolde's Tower (Exchange St Lower)
- fish and vegetable carvings on Fruit & Veg Market
- The Church pub

REFRESHMENTS: The Church (01-828-0102; www.thechurch.ie) – junction of Mary St and Jervis St.

INFORMATION:

Dublin Tourism Centre: Suffolk St, Dublin 2 (www.visitdublin.com).

Pat Liddy's Walking Tours of Dublin: 087-252-6701 or 085-905-2480; www.walking-tours.ie. Private groups/individuals: enquire about prices. Scheduled tours (6 per day) from €5, 1 May–31 October, from Dublin Tourism Centre, Suffolk St.

iWalks (www.visitdublin.com): Download free podcast audio guides, with Pat Liddy's commentary guiding you round the city.

17
HOWTH PENINSULA, CO DUBLIN

A BEAUTIFUL LATE WINTER'S morning, cold and blue. Outside Howth DART station I met a bunch of friends and relations, all raring to explore the cliff paths of the bulbous peninsula. It was great to have enthusiastic younger folk along for the walk. Sisters Katie (12) and Hannah (10) from the south side of Dublin Bay, fine talkers and walkers, were out to show their English cousins Michael and Elizabeth the cream of the country. At 13 years old, Michael was all for everything; his 16-year-old sister, more of a cat that walks by herself, stalked ahead as outrider for our party.

A twin-masted sailing boat was negotiating the long stag-beetle jaws of Howth Harbour, putting me in mind of the extraordinary events of July 1914 when Erskine Childers sailed into this port in his stout little yacht *Asgard* with 900 rifles and 25,000 rounds for the use of the Irish Volunteers. The historic yacht's namesake, the Arklow-built brigantine *Asgard II*, went down in the Bay of Biscay in September 2008, and now lies full fathom five for ever more – a sad end for a much-loved training vessel.

Before venturing out along the cliffs, we detoured up above the harbour to catch the view around the ruins of Howth

Collegiate and Abbey, and to pay our respects to the shade of Father Patrick, legendary teacher at the ecclesiastical college in medieval times. It's said that French rivals, jealous of the college's fame and success, came to Howth confident of finding enough evidence of dire teaching to force its closure. But cunning Father Patrick had planted his learned monks around the harbour disguised as working men. The disembarking spies heard fish porters and roadmenders discussing recondite theological matters in Latin, got back on board and sailed away dumbfounded.

Beyond the Martello Tower we passed above the broad curve of Balscadden Bay and were out along the Nose of Howth in no time, with wonderful views to the north over the green sister islands of Ireland's Eye and Lambay. Cries from the children, scampering ahead on the narrow path, drew my eyes to a seal close inshore, bobbing in the water like a fat bald man in a wetsuit as he watched a fisherman take up his catch. Big dark P&O ferries trod heavily out to sea through a great smeary patch of silver laid along the water by the low winter sun.

The path ran through heather and gorse, a brown ribbon easy to follow. We had a chocolate break sitting on a bench in the sun, where the talk turned to music (Katie and Hannah are both traditional players) and football (Elizabeth and Michael have Chelsea Blue all through them like two sticks of rock). Then it was up and on, with a most tremendous southward view steadily widening over the peninsula's stumpy white Baily Lighthouse, out across the great arc of Dublin Bay where the wind was wrinkling the sea like leviathan hide, to a graceful line of blue mountain peaks 20 miles off in mist-hazed Wicklow.

Past the lighthouse and the exotic sub-tropical gardens of handsome cliff-top residences, we dropped down to Doldrum Bay. The adults lay nibbling and chatting on a knoll, while the three youngest cousins dashed down to the shore and climbed all the sea stacks they could get their hands on. Energy like that, distilled and bottled, could make someone's fortune.

Now the path struck inland, looping through head-high thickets of gorse on the lower slopes of Shielmartin. I remembered climbing up there on another blowy cold day to find the ring of white quartzite boulders marking the tomb of the warrior king Crimhthan Niadhnair. Assisted by his wife, the goddess Nar of the Brugh, he brought vast plunder back to Ireland from raids against Roman Britain, and buried it . . . who knows where? Such stories are the very stuff of the land we walk on. Down the hill in Howth Demesne lies a great portal dolmen with a 100-ton capstone. Some tales say it is a memorial to beautiful Aideen, dead of a broken heart after her beloved husband Oscar fell fighting near Tara. Or is it a quoit thrown here from the Bog of Allen by the mighty arm of Fionn MacCumhaill?

Back in Howth, I considered taking the children on to see the dolmen; then looked at their faces, a little tired now, and thought better of it. Chips and ice-cream were on their minds now. You'd better not argue with those.

ASGARD

IRELAND'S EYE

HOWTH HARBOUR

HOWTH STATION
(DART)
START & FINISH

BALSCADDEN BAY

HOWTH CASTLE

NOSE OF HOWTH

HOWTH CASTLE

HOWTH ABBEY

HOWTH

OPTIONAL DETOUR

RESERVOIR

AIDEEN'S GRAVE

CAIRN OF CRIMHTHAN NIADHNAIR

BOG OF FROGS

BEN OF HOWTH

SHIELMARTIN

HOWTH GOLF COURSE

GORSE-LINED PATH

DOLDRUM BAY

BAILY LIGHTHOUSE

HOWTH PENINSULA, DUBLIN

WAY TO GO

MAP: OS of Ireland 1:50,000 Discovery 50; downloadable map/instructions at www.discoverireland.ie/walking.

TRAVEL:

Rail: DART to Howth.

Road: M50 to Jct 3, N32, on to Howth.

WALK DIRECTIONS (waymarked with purple arrows): From DART station, left along Howth Harbour (detour right up Abbey Street to Collegiate ruin, then right again up Church Street for Howth Abbey). Continue along harbour, then follow purple arrows for 4 miles along cliffs, past Baily Lighthouse and on past Doldrum Bay. Just short of Martello Tower, bear right inland (purple arrows) to cross Carrickbrack Road. Follow purple arrows through gorse, over golf course (white stone path markers) and on through Bog of Frogs. Bear left downhill through Balkill Park estate to Howth DART station. (Detour: left along road for 400 m to find gates to Howth Castle, Howth Demesne and Aideen's Grave.)

LENGTH: 6½ miles: allow 3 hours.

GRADE: Easy/Moderate

CONDITIONS: Some muddy patches between Baily lighthouse and Doldrum Bay; otherwise fair underfoot.

DON'T MISS:
- Howth Collegiate and Abbey
- view from eastern cliffs over lighthouse, Dublin Bay and Wicklow Hills
- beaches around Doldrum Bay for picnics and a scamper

REFRESHMENTS:

Abbey Tavern, Abbey Road, Howth (01-839-0307; www.abbeytavern.ie) – fires, comfort, good bar food.

La Cucina, Harbour Road (01-832-4443; www.wrightsfindlaterhowth.com) – family-friendly place.

INFORMATION: www.visitdublin.com.

18

DONADEA FOREST PARK, CO KILDARE

THE DETERMINED LADY IN very short shorts leaped from her car and bounced away as if on springs under the dripping horse chestnuts of Donadea Forest Park. That was our first 'serious pelter' sighting of the day, and not the last by any means. Most of the competitors in the Donadea 10K race, though, seemed happy to take things at a rather steadier pace. In twos, fives and tens they went trotting off down the leaf-strewn path, arms pumping, adrenaline a-squirt.

The ladies and gentlemen of Donadea Running Club weren't the only folk out and about among the chestnuts and beeches this morning. Situated where it is, less than an hour's drive east of Dublin in the gently rolling landscape of north Kildare, the former estate of the Aylmer family has become a powerful magnet for outdoor enthusiasts in its present guise as Donadea Forest Park. Coillte manages ten of these Forest Parks across the country, and with their multiple facilities, well surfaced waymarked routes and family-friendly atmosphere, they've proved a big hit with walkers from toddlers to yompers, as well as with kite-flyers, tai-chi'ites, kickabouters, and the sprinters who gallop their paths.

As soon as Jane and I had got in among the woods ourselves, there wasn't a sound to be heard. The panting and pounding runners might have been in another world – Planet Pain, probably. We trod a carpet of rich golden beech leaves under trees that steamed the vapour of yesterday's downpours. Stands of rosebay willowherb, iconic plant of disturbed ground, showed tall spiky stalks, the pinky-purple flowers so eye-catching in summer – now shrunk away to nothing, the pale green of each spear-blade leaf edged with the dull gold of vegetable decay.

'Eerie light,' said Jane, exploring the undergrowth. 'Grimm's fairy tales!' Brackens spread their peacock tails, hart's tongues crinkled in the gloom. A mossy stump stood half-rotted, its velvety table piled with the tempting-looking fungi called Granny's Cakes. Brambles, leaf-mould and subtly gleaming fungi exhaled the dark, fruity smell that tells of deep old winter not far off.

It was hard to believe we were sharing these woods with 600 runners, until we rounded a corner and found them bearing right down on us. A bunch of tightly muscled greyhounds at first; then a whole river of runners in flood. We stood right back and let them pass, sweating, snorting, grimacing, doing their best and then some. The strong whiff of hard-worked horseflesh hung in the air. A wheezing, malodorous, steaming army, but admirable, even enviable, for all that. One little lad, spotting his uncle, suddenly leaped up in the air beside me, smacking his palms together and squealing out, 'Go, Barney! Come on, Barney! Only six to go!' I wouldn't have been surprised to see Barney, struggling and well back in the field, fall dead on hearing that. Instead he dredged up a watery smile and raised a tremulous thumb.

After the runners had passed we went on, through woods once more wrapped in silence. Round another bend we came on Competitor 332, a tiny baby slung in front of his mother and kicking fit to beat the band. Beyond stood the runners' friends and relations, water bottles and bananas at the ready, waiting beside a pair of dark stone obelisks – a memorial to the dead of 9/11. McMahon, O'Rourke, Leahy, Callahan, Farrelly: no need to ask where so many of the Twin Towers

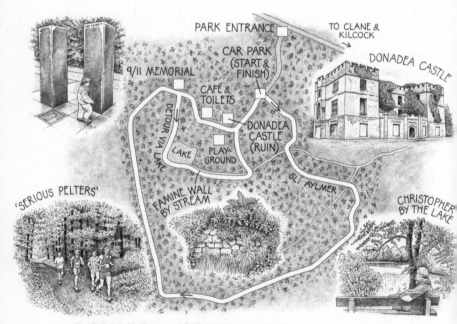

DONADEA FOREST PARK, CO. KILDARE

victims had their family origins. Perhaps some of their ancestors were those who, in the Famine years, built stone walls along the streams through the Aylmer estate to earn their bread.

We rounded the lake and came by the derelict hulk of Donadea Castle, unroofed in the 1950s and left to rot. Blank windows crowded with ivy, battlements shaggy with bushes, gated and barred, the Gothic house seemed a desert island amid the waves of cheerful runners, their families and friends, all streaming away laughing and teasing at the end of the race.

Ah, the results? Mick Coyle won in 0.34.10, beating his nearest rival by a pretty whopping seven seconds. Baby 332 came in . . . well, 520th from First, let's say. And last of all was . . . Hmmm, quite honestly, a gentleman shouldn't tell. And this one won't.

WAY TO GO

MAP: OS of Ireland 1:50,000 Discovery 49; downloadable map/instructions at www.discoverireland.ie/walking.

TRAVEL:

Rail (www.irishrail.ie): Nearest station Enfield (10 miles).

Bus (www.buseireann.ie): 120 Dublin–Prosperous (5 miles).

Road: M4 to Kilcock, R407 towards Clane/Naas; in 4 miles, left at Baltracey crossroads to Donadea Forest Park (signed). Entrance fee: bring €5 in coins.

WALK DIRECTIONS: From car park cross tarred roadway and pass barrier. Follow 'Sli Aylmer' red arrows clockwise around Forest Park for 2½ miles to 9/11 memorial on left. Right here down Sean Tallon Way; follow red arrows round lake and on ('Nature Trail' fingerpost), to pass Donadea Castle and return to car park.

LENGTH: 4 miles: allow 2 hours.

GRADE: Easy

CONDITIONS: Surfaced paths.

DON'T MISS:
- 9/11 Memorial
- Famine walls along streams
- Donadea Castle

REFRESHMENTS: Forest Park café.

INFORMATION:

Tourist Office: Kildare Town Heritage Centre, Market Square, Kildare; 045-530672; www.kildare.ie/kildareheritage.

19

TULLAMORE TO BALLYCOMMON BRIDGE, GRAND CANAL, CO OFFALY

'YOU'LL HAVE A BRILLIANT time along the Grand Canal today,' offered Rose Mooney in the Tourist Office at Tullamore Dew Heritage Centre. 'A bit of sun, nice dry path and some beautiful country, especially if you head out for Ballycommon. Hungry? Just down those steps in the café – you won't do better anywhere!'

How right Rose was. Delicious, crispy, oven-baked focaccia: now that's something you'd have struggled to find in deepest Offaly not so long ago. Jane and I stepped out replete into a gorgeous sunny afternoon under gently whispering poplars, just the kind of thing that makes you long to head for the hayfield with a jar of cider.

It was another drop of the good stuff that brought fame to Tullamore once the Grand Canal had reached the town at the end of the 18th century. Tullamore Dew became one of the world's best-selling whiskeys, a rich and fiery concoction. It's made at Midleton, Co Cork these days; the handsome old bonded warehouse in Tullamore now houses the Heritage Centre, and the canal still passes the door.

What a truly grand conception was the Grand Canal – a mighty thread for commerce and communication clean across the waist of Ireland for the best part of 100 miles from Dublin to the Shannon, Irish Sea to Atlantic Ocean. It throve for half a century until the railways pinched most of its business. Nowadays the old waterway is alive with fish, frogs, birds, butterflies, wild flowers and dragonflies. You can sail it or bike it or walk it. The Offaly boglands are flat, and flat is beautiful in this context.

Water lily pads floated on the wind-ruffled water. Yellow flags raised their large papery flowers from clumps of rush and sedge. The canal arrowed away under its hump-backed bridges. A timeless, pastoral scene, rudely invaded by two flashing and beeping fire engines and half a dozen gallant gentlemen of the Fire Brigade. 'There was a horse got himself stuck over a gate,' disclosed a firefighter, with all the pride of one who has saved a princess from a blazing citadel, 'but we got him off it, no trouble to him.' The piebald horse himself lay in the recovery position a little further down the bank, rather pink around the gills, his eyes closed, waiting for all the nasty stuff to go far away.

At Boland's Lock the Round House jutted towards the canal, a lock-keeper's house rather grander than any other with its castellated gable and elliptical shape. The contractor who built it, Michael Hayes, just went ahead and created something that pleased him, but the board of directors of the Grand Canal weren't *that* grand.

Unimpressed by Hayes's extravagance, they refused to pay his extra bill for the fancy bits – all £42.7.11d of it.

Pushing the canal through the soft, sucking peat bogs of the Midlands was a huge undertaking. It took five years just to cross the Bog of Allen. Coals, clothes, wood, crockery, wool, groceries, spare parts, beer, whiskey, people – the canal carried them all across Ireland. Now this former traffic artery sees the occasional boat, a scatter of anglers, some strollers such as ourselves, and one or two runners pink to the cheeks with exertion.

Electric blue damselflies hovered over the lily pads. Through the clear water we saw lazily waving weeds shaped like lettuces, like ash tree fronds, like strawberry flowers. There were genuine wild strawberries to pick and savour among the early purple orchids and yellow-headed black medick. Common twayblade

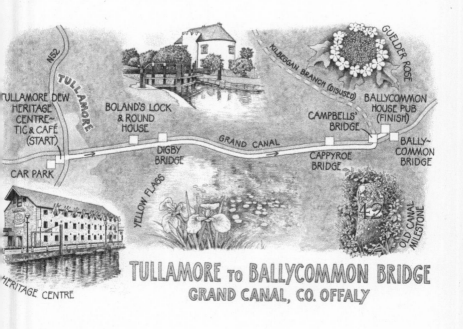

TULLAMORE TO BALLYCOMMON BRIDGE
GRAND CANAL, CO. OFFALY

grew in patches, each tall spike of green flowers like a tower of tiny acrobats in turbans and long baggy slave pants. A great spider with a body ribbed in brilliant green segments let me get close with the camera, then scrambled across its high wire thread and out of sight.

The leaky lock gates near Cappyroe Bridge spurted jets of water a dozen ways at once. We crossed Campbells' Bridge across the overgrown bed of the former canal branch to Kilbeggan, and came to the pub by the bridge at Ballycommon. Anyone trying to coax a gallon out of the venerable petrol pump here would have their work cut out. But it made a fine spot to sit and talk over the walk while we waited for the taxi.

WAY TO GO

MAP: OS of Ireland 1:50,000 Discovery 48; www.discoverireland.ie/walking; strip map in *Guide to the Grand Canal of Ireland* (see below).

TRAVEL:

Rail (www.irishrail.ie): to Tullamore.

Bus (www.buseireann.ie): Service 120 Dublin–Tullamore.

Road: N6, N52. Car park just beyond TIC.

WALK DIRECTIONS: From TIC and Tullamore Dew Heritage Centre, turn right and follow canal to Ballycommon Bridge. Ballycommon House PH is on left (north) bank, just beyond Lock 21. Return: taxi (057-932-1777 or 057-932-2225).

LENGTH: 5½ miles: allow 2–3 hours.

GRADE: Easy

CONDITIONS: Grass path on right (south) bank; dirt track or tarmac road on left (north).

DON'T MISS:
- Tullamore Dew Heritage Centre
- Round House at Boland's Lock
- wild flowers (bring a hand lens and flower book)

REFRESHMENTS: Tullamore Dew Heritage Centre café – superb cooking.

INFORMATION:

Good advice on walking Grand Canal: www.grandcanalhike.org.

Tourist Office: Tullamore Dew Heritage Centre, Bury Quay; 093-25015;

www.tullamore-dew.org; www.discoverireland.ie/Shannon.

Guide to the Grand Canal of Ireland by Ruth Delany and Jeremy Addis (Dúchas) – available in Tullamore TIC.

20

GLENBARROW AND THE RIDGE OF CAPARD, SLIEVE BLOOM MOUNTAINS, CO LAOIS

THERE'S SOMETHING MYSTERIOUS, HALF-INVISIBLE even, about the Slieve Blooms. These low-rolling hills, rising at the meeting point of Laois and Offaly, are only an hour from Dublin on a good traffic day. But mention them to most people, and you'll get a puzzled shrug. Partly the modesty of the Slieve Blooms' public image is down to the fact that they rise from the huge empty expanse of the flat Midlands plain, not a location that most folk would think of as walking country; partly it's that they fall between hills and mountains in their height and scope. Yet local walkers are fanatical in their devotion; the Slieve Blooms have one of the best walking festivals in Ireland, and one of the keenest and friendliest walking clubs.

It's hard to believe that such a compact range could hold so many secret valleys and hidden rivers. Glenbarrow is a great example. According to Slieve Bloom myths the Barrow is a river with a furious spirit, capable of apocalyptic floods if its wellhead is interfered with – or even glanced upon. Once roused, the angry waters could only be appeased by being sprinkled with milk from the hand of a virgin priest (they weren't all, you know).

There was no such rage in the river today. In the narrow cleft of Glenbarrow it rushed shallow and peat-brown through the forest. We walked a pine needle carpet through cathedral-like conifers where long-tailed tits gave out their thin little call, *zee-zee-zee*, and tiny goldcrests skimmed on white-barred wings from one perch to the next.

Down by the river we ventured out on the jumbled grey boulders and shallow red rock plates of the riverbed. Here the River Barrow pours through the cracks and joints in the soft sandstone, cutting itself miniature waterfalls and foot-high cascades. The sandstone slabs reflect the movement of the river in their many-leaved, blade-thin strata, rippling back from the leading edges like fossilised wavelets. A perfect picnic spot for children to splash and explore, though slippery enough for a bit of care.

A little further along the path we came to a viewpoint where Clamphole Falls came jumping down a series of rock steps in fans of hissing water. A dipper flew up and perched on the rim of the waterfall, its white breast shining like a torch as it bobbed up and down. A flutter of wings and it had dived into the upper pool, to walk upstream underwater in search of caddis-flies and tiny freshwater snails among the stones.

From the falls we followed the trail as it rose out of the trees among wild strawberry (plump, sweet and ripe for picking) and bilberry (on the way there, but still a bit green). Speckled wood butterflies spread themselves among the grasses, opening their beautiful wings of velvet brown with sherbet-yellow spots to catch the sun. The beaked pink flowers of lousewort and the royal blue petals of milkwort studded the open heather, and the gorse in full bloom blazed as brilliant gold as any burning bush.

The view from the crest of the Ridge of Capard was absolutely sensational. Standing in a sea of wind-rippled bog cotton we stared round a complete circle – east as far as the Wicklow Mountains, south to what looked like a squeak of the Comeraghs, Knockmealdowns and Galtees, and north across the brown and green patchwork of the great Midlands plain. In past accounts of walks I have been taken to task by readers for over-estimation after describing '100-mile-views' which probably aren't quite that. So all I'll say of the Ridge of Capard is that it gives a prospect fit to make you sing. And we did – 'I Can See For Miles', at the top of our voices.

A crunchy forest road and a stumbly path over knotty tree roots returned us to the car, our heads full of views, our fingers sticky with lemon-scented pine resin.

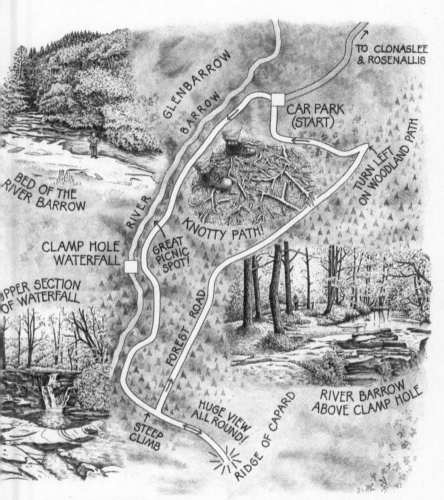

TO CLONASLEE & ROSENALLIS

GLENBARROW BARROW

CAR PARK (START)

TURN LEFT ON WOODLAND PATH

KNOTTY PATH!

BED OF THE RIVER BARROW

RIVER

CLAMP HOLE WATERFALL

GREAT PICNIC SPOT!

UPPER SECTION OF WATERFALL

FOREST ROAD

STEEP CLIMB

HUGE VIEW ALL ROUND!

RIDGE OF CAPARD

RIVER BARROW ABOVE CLAMP HOLE

GLENBARROW & THE RIDGE OF CAPARD
SLIEVE BLOOM MOUNTAINS, CO. LAOIS

WAY TO GO

MAP: OS of Ireland 1:50,000 Discovery 54; downloadable map/instructions (highly recommended) at www.discoverireland.ie/walking.

TRAVEL:

Rail (www.irishrail.ie): Portlaoise (11 miles).

Bus (www.buseireann.ie): Clonaslee–Rosenallis–Mountmellick–Dublin service under consideration (info: 057-8692168).

ROAD: Side road to Glenbarrow signposted off R422 (Clonaslee–Mountmellick), on bend in Rosenallis. First right, then first left to Glenbarrow car park.

WALK DIRECTIONS: Follow Blue Route ('Waterfall'; blue arrows/BA). 500 m beyond Clamp Hole waterfall, Blue Route climbs to meet forest road. Cross and climb path (yellow arrows) to Ridge of Capard (superb views). Return to forest road; turn right (BAs). In 1 mile, another forest road rises to right; turn left here (BAs) down forest path, back to car park.

LENGTH: 4 miles: allow 2 hours.

GRADE: Moderate

CONDITIONS: Rocks, tree roots underfoot; short sections boggy and steep. Slippery rocks along river. Buggy-friendly along forest roads.

DON'T MISS:
- Clamphole Falls
- wild strawberries and bilberries in season on way up to Ridge of Capard
- view from the ridge

REFRESHMENTS: None en route – picnic.

INFORMATION:

Portlaoise Tourist Information Office: James Fintan Lawlor Avenue (057-862-1178); www.midirelandtourism.ie.

Bladhma by Tom Joyce (Acorn Press).

Slieve Bloom Guided Walks: visit http://www.slievebloom.ie/walking_programme. html; 086-278-9147; info@slievebloom.ie.

ALL WALKING INFO: www.slievebloom.ie.

21

River Shannon, Errina Canal and the Headrace, O'Briensbridge, Co Clare

'THE FLOODS CAME UP to here,' said Michael Murtagh, chairman of the O'Briensbridge Community Group, laying his hand on a willow branch five feet above the towpath. 'We'd never known the Shannon do that before!'

No one who witnessed the floods on the River Shannon along the Clare/Limerick border in November 2009 will soon forget the spectacle. There were fears that the 14 arches of the bridge at O'Briensbridge might give way before the brown torrent released from Lough Derg that seethed and spouted through them. Trees went sailing, fields disappeared, gardens were inundated. It seemed an apocalyptic event. Yet, Michael revealed as we strolled downriver from pretty O'Briensbridge, things had regularly been as bad as that – or worse – before the Electricity Supply Board dammed the Shannon's outfall from Lough Derg at Parteen Weir.

'They opened Parteen Weir in 1929

and sent two-thirds of the water down a new canal – we call it the Headrace – to feed the hydro-electric scheme at Ardnacrusha, just outside Limerick. That tamed the Shannon. Before then the river level was much, much higher, and it was all low-lying bogland each side. Oh, you'd have had powerful flooding back then, all right!'

Michael Murtagh should know all about the Shannon and its many moods. He worked for the ESB developing fisheries, creating habitats for fish and birds, and making spawning beds for the wild salmon whose route to their native streams has been blocked by developments along the river. The looped walk we were following down the Shannon, along its tributary Errina Canal and back along the Headrace, was planned and laid out with the expert help and advice of the O'Briensbridge Community Group and its ever-enthusiastic chairman. Michael just can't keep himself away from his beloved Shannon, and no one with eyes and ears could blame him. In this part of the world, snaking as a wide ribbon of molten bronze and silver between the contiguous counties of Clare, Limerick and Tipperary, overhung with trees, slow flowing and majestic, the Shannon is a kingly river and a beautiful one.

A mile out of O'Briensbridge we spied a curious procession approaching along the bank. Two men, a woman, and a brace of dogs leaping crazily – and small wonder, for one of the men had a large muddy swan cradled in his arms. 'Taking it to the vet,' he said laconically. The big bird lay against his chest as if stunned, its large coarse-skinned feet dangling, its long neck curved in a hoop as its protector shielded its eyes with one hand to prevent it seeing the slavering muzzles of the dogs as they jumped, mad with bravado and excitement.

110

Now we swung away from the shining Shannon and made inland along the tree-shaded towpath of the long-abandoned Errina Canal. 'My favourite part of the walk,' murmured Michael. 'I love the peace of it, out in the country under the trees like this.'

Barges, like salmon, cannot easily negotiate obstacles in the river, and the canal was built in the 1780s to bypass the salmon fishery at Castleconnell. Today all was quiet along the old canal. Among the bushes of Rose of Sharon with their plump inky fruit we found exotically striped yellow and orange snails as bright and shiny as sweets. At Errina Bridge we stooped to inspect the grooves that barge ropes had gouged as the horses dragged them decade after decade against the stone bridge abutments. Then it was up on to the long smooth curve of the Headrace embankment, walking against the water's flow.

A quick detour to Michael's house for a sandwich and a cup of tea, and we strode on along the Headrace towards Lough Derg, Michael's bouncy little dog Jack at our heels ('part Jack Russell, part eejit!'). Stupendous views opened to the billowing heights of Slieve Bernagh and the tall, eye-catching dome of Keeper Hill, still patched with winter snow. Up at the castle-like edifice of Parteen Weir we lingered, stunned by the sight and sound of white water jetting thunderously through the sluices, till the slanting light of a cold sunset made us shiver and bend our steps to the homeward path.

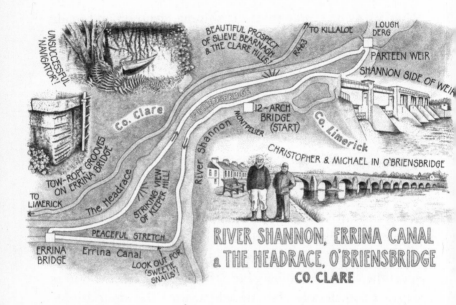

UNSUCCESSFUL 'NAVIGATOR'!

BEAUTIFUL PROSPECT OF SLIEVE BEARNAGH & THE CLARE HILLS.

TO KILLALOE

LOUGH DERG

R463

PARTEEN WEIR

SHANNON SIDE OF WEIR

Co. Clare

O'BRIENSBRIDGE

12~ARCH BRIDGE (START)

MONTPELIER

River Shannon

Co. Limerick

CHRISTOPHER & MICHAEL IN O'BRIENSBRIDGE

TOW-ROPE GROOVES ON ERRINA BRIDGE

The Headrace

STRIKING VIEW OF KEEPER HILLS

TO LIMERICK

PEACEFUL STRETCH

ERRINA BRIDGE

Errina Canal

LOOK OUT FOR 'SWEETIE SNAILS'!

RIVER SHANNON, ERRINA CANAL & THE HEADRACE, O'BRIENSBRIDGE
CO. CLARE

WAY TO GO

MAP: OS of Ireland 1:50,000 Discovery 58; downloadable map/instructions at www.discoverireland.ie/walking.

TRAVEL:

Rail (www.irishrail.ie): Castleconnell or Birdhill (both 5 miles).

Bus (www.buseireann.ie): 323, 345.

Road: On R463 Limerick–Killaloe; off N7 Limerick–Nenagh.

WALK DIRECTIONS: From bridge at O'Briensbridge follow Shannon towpath (blue arrows/BA) downstream on right bank. In 1½ miles bear right along Errina Canal towpath. In 1 mile go under Errina Bridge; climb up to road; left (BA) along road; through gate (BA); right along right bank of the Headrace for 2¾ miles to Parteen Weir. Descend slope with handrail on right; follow Parteen Weir Loop (green arrows) downstream beside Shannon to O'Briensbridge.

LENGTH: 7½ miles: allow 3 hours.

GRADE: Easy

DON'T MISS:

- views of O'Briensbridge from Shannon towpath
- tow-rope grooves on Errina Bridge
- Parteen Weir and views over Lough Derg

REFRESHMENTS: Old Mill Bar & Restaurant, O'Briensbridge (061-372299/372020; http://www.vfi.ie/Pub/18-The-Old-Mill).

ACCOMMODATION: Anvil B&B, Smithy's Place, Montpelier, O'Briensbridge (061-372005).

INFORMATION:

Tourist Office: Arthur's Row, Ennis; 065-682-8366; www.shannonregiontourism.ie.

Contact Michael Murtagh (061-377289/ 086-856-6556).

22

MULLAGHMORE, THE BURREN, CO CLARE

T HERE'S DEFINITELY SOME MAGIC about the Burren region of County Clare – the naked limestone hills so packed with wildlife, yet so seemingly empty; the bare grey landscape that hides a fabulous treasury of archaeological sites; the sleepy one-tractor villages where music springs at full flow from plain-looking pubs. When you fall in love with this mysterious place, you fall hard. The first time I clapped eyes on Mullaghmore in the south-east corner of the region, 20 years ago, I reckoned it my favourite hill in all the world, and I haven't changed my mind since.

Now that the Burren National Park has laid out a modest but excellently waymarked network of paths over Mullaghmore, there's no need to scramble up the fractured cliffs by the tips of your fingers. But nothing can tame this magnificent swirl of contorted limestone. When you glimpse it first, you gasp and wonder if you're seeing things. It's as if a giant has grabbed Mullaghmore and its neighbouring peak of Sliabh Rua and given them a vigorous twist. They curl and bend in a way that stone just isn't supposed to do. They beckon you to explore.

Setting off from a lane in the back of beyond north of Kilnaboy, Jane and I skirted Lough Gealáin at the foot of the hill. A turlough or seasonal lake, it lay half-dried, its shores and shallows powdered with lime dust over which the water shone a clear Mediterranean turquoise. We squelched out on to the mud and were rewarded with the spectacle of the biggest, baddest black leech you ever did see.

Up on the slopes of Mullaghmore the grey limestone was alive with wild flowers. One of the Burren's many magicalities is the way that lime-loving and acid-loving flowers cosy up together. Flora of the heights grows contentedly at sea level; plants of the low places flourish halfway up the hills. The sun-warmed stone, the damp and shelter in the cracks called grykes, the acid seeps and calcareous drips all conspire to allow the heather to lie down with the gentian, and the bog asphodel with the primrose.

Jane, the trained botanist, was in heaven, kneeling among crinkly yellow rockrose and the creamy porcelain-thin cups of mountain avens, musing over orchids that might be early purples in late flower or pyramidals at some other stage. I walked slowly, enjoying the buzz-saw symphony of grasshoppers and bees. A slender bar of neon as long as my little finger materialised beside me, then vanished, to reappear five feet off – a damselfly, as brilliantly blue as a kingfisher's back.

The walk at this lower level was a series of small, intimate images. A peregrine falcon chittering away, a dark and deadly little hunter flashing along the pale grey cliffs. A silver-washed fritillary butterfly settling on a rock to sun its leopard-spotted wings. Two crimson and black cinnabar moths mating on a grass stalk. A purple flower of bloody cranesbill collapsing under the weight of a corpulent bumble bee.

115

Shards of dry limestone clinked like china underfoot. We climbed the faint trail up miniature passes in the crags, the reflected heat from the limestone beginning to flush our necks and cheeks, to top out by the pointed summit cairn. Now for the view over the grey sweep of the Burren landscape, the lime-crusted turloughs like flakes of abalone, the hidden spirals and vortices of rock that you'll never see except from up here on the roof of Mullaghmore.

On the north slope we stopped to savour the full measure of the strangeness of Sliabh Rua and its thick twists of limestone, as though an ash-coloured boa constrictor had wrapped its coils round the neck of the secondary hill. Then it was back along the western slopes. Glancing across the valley, Jane suddenly exclaimed: 'Father Ted's house!' So it

MULLAGHMORE, THE BURREN, CO. CLARE

was, unmistakeably: standing back on its own, square and grey, with that familiar white front door. A great thirst for a cup of tea suddenly descended on us. 'Ah, you will!' we said simultaneously, and burst out giggling.

WAY TO GO

MAP: OS of Ireland 1:50,000 Discovery 52; Folding Landscapes map 'The Burren' (www.foldinglandscapes.com); Burren National Park Walking Trails map, available from Burren Centre, Kilfenora, or downloadable at www.shannonregiontrails.ie.

TRAVEL:

Rail (www.irishrail.ie): Ennis (10 miles).

Bus (www.buseireann.ie): Service 333 (Ennis–Doonbeg), 337 (Ennis–Doolin) to Corofin (5 miles).

Road: R476 Corofin–Kilnaboy; right ('school and church') for 3 miles. Pass parking layby with noticeboard on right; in 100 m, right. In ¾ mile, park by yellow 'walking man' waymark and Burren National Park noticeboard on left.

WALK DIRECTIONS: Through stone stile; follow blue arrows around south shore of Lough Gealáin, up Mullaghmore to summit cairn, round north end and back along western slopes.

LENGTH: 4 miles: allow 2–3 hours.

GRADE: Moderate/Hard

CONDITIONS: Rough and wobbly underfoot; stout trainers/boots. Well marked; binoculars useful for spotting distant waymarks.

DON'T MISS:
- glorious spread of wildflowers
- view from north end of Mullaghmore over Sliabh Rua
- view of 'Father Ted's house' at Glenquin, from western slopes

REFRESHMENTS: None en route – take a picnic.

Cont.

INFORMATION:

Ennis Tourist Office: Arthur's Row, O'Connell Square; 065-682-8366; www.clare.ie www.discoverireland.ie/shannon.

Burren National Park: 01-888-2000; www.burrennationalpark.ie.

Burren Centre, Kilfenora: 065-708-8030; www.theburrencentre.ie.

Burren Guided Walks and Hikes with Mary Howard (065-707-6100/ 087-244-6807 www.burrenguidedwalks.com).

23

BLACK HEAD LOOP, THE BURREN, CO CLARE

THE VIOLET THROATS OF self heal open along the grassy verges of the Caher River, overlooked by yellow rattle's parrot beaks of seedheads. Sulphur-coloured lady's bedstraw peeping from a gryke, a shadowed slit in the limestone pavement. Rarer-than-hens'-teeth Irish saxifrage, an acid-loving plant, in the hollow of a clint, or natural cobble, of pure limestone. Everywhere the diminutive white peepers of eyebright. Domed grey hills that frame a slaty blue sea flecked with whitecaps. Field walls of axe-blade stones delicately balanced, so that the sky shines through in blue and silver like a celestial stained-glass window. Where else but the Burren region of north-west Clare?

You could rummage around in this botanical jewel-case for the simple pleasure of bedazzlement by colour, shape and scent – especially with one of Tim Robinson's incomparable 'Folding Landscape' maps to hand. But on this windy morning, walking a shortened version of the Black Head loop, Jane and I were lucky enough to have the company of Mary Howard, a Burren resident and devotee who really knows her plants. 'Field scabious,' she said, sweeping her hand across the blue powder-puff flowers as we climbed the narrow road up the Caher Valley. 'Bloody cranesbill in this lower grassland – I love that deep winey colour. Oh, and look – grass of Parnassus!' A cup of slender, porcelain-white petals with delicate green veins rose from the rocks. 'Now that *is* gorgeous!'

I dipped my beak into a fragrant orchid – a faint and pungent smell, more like a nice piece of steak than a flower. A beautiful, orange-and-black chequered butterfly skimmed a clump of nodding harebells. 'Pearl bordered fritillary,' Mary murmured. 'Everyone we take walking loves those.'

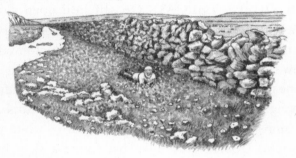

People adore the incomparable Burren landscape, especially when they're exploring on foot. 'My husband Gerry and I love walking, so we got into providing walking holidays for small groups. It started as just one weekend in March, but ended that year with every weekend busy till October! I get such a mix of people who are interested in so many things, literally from cloud formations down to the smallest flower and insect.'

There were Connemara ponies on the skyline and goats on the limestone terraces, white, black and brown against grey stone and blue sky. Up on the ridge between Caher and Rathborney Rivers we explored the ruin of Cathair an Aird Rois, a ring fort of wind-tight walls enclosing the crumbling shells of a Mass house and a shebeen – the Lord and the Devil, cheek by jowl. Over on Poulanegh Hill I filled my water bottle from a sweet spring under a fuchsia bush. 'Deora Dé, the Tears of God,' said Mary, indicating the flowers hanging like scarlet and purple lanterns.

Wild flowers spattered rock and sward, as if a mad painter had dipped his thickest brush in every pot and flicked it all over the land. We found pale pink squinancywort – 'A cure for a smoky throat!' – and mountain avens, a creamy bowl of petals with an intense yellow centre. 'The summer is wonderful for them. You look over Black Head, and it's carpeted like snow.'

Towards evening we dropped down a concertina path, and followed an old drove road back along the cliffs of Black Head. 'I had ten American poets on a walk along here,' Mary reminisced. 'You should have seen the arm waving and striking of poses – marvellous!'

The Burren was holding back two very special botanical treats. Almost at the end of our walk we found them – Irish eyebright on a long bronze stalk, and the very beautiful white spiral of autumn lady's tresses. Raising my eyes from ground level to watch the sun dip seaward over the Aran Islands, I knew this was a little slice of heaven on earth.

BLACK HEAD LOOP
THE BURREN
CO. CLARE

BLACK HEAD

MARY HOWARD
NEAR CATHAIR
AN AIRD ROIS

OLD DROVE ROAD~
SENSATIONAL VIEWS TO
ARAN ISLANDS

PEARL BORDERED
FRITILLARY

QUAY

JUNGLY BIT!

TO
BALLYVAUGHAN

AGHAGLINNY
NORTH

R477

* FOLLOW PURPLE
ARROWS ACROSS
ROUGH, ROCKY
GROUND

FANORE
BRIDGE

GLENINAGH
MOUNTAIN

WILD FLOWERS A-GOGO!

POULANEGI
HILL

FANORE
BEACH
CAR
PARK~
(START &
FINISH)

Caher River

KHYBER PASS

R477

CATHAIR AN
AIRD ROIS

MOUNTAIN
AVENS &
AUTUMN
LADY'S
TRESSES

COMPLETE BLACK HEAD LOOP
(16 MILES)

CHRISTOPHER HUNTS
FOR ORCHIDS

122

WAY TO GO

MAP: OS of Ireland 1:50,000 Discovery 51; downloadable map/instructions (highly recommended) at www.discoverireland.ie/walking.

TRAVEL:

Bus (www.buseireann.ie): Galway–Ballyvaughan–Cliffs of Moher, Services 423, 050.

Road: From Galway – N18, N67 to Ballyvaughan; R477 to Fanore. Park in Fanore beach car park.

WALK DIRECTIONS: Left along R477 (*take care!*) for ½ mile; right at Fanore bridge (OSI ref. M 145089) up side road for 2½ miles. Pass turning on right (174069; 'Burren Way/BW'); in 30 m, left up track (BW; yellow 'walking man'; purple arrow/ 'PA), past Cathair an Aird Rois, down to road (190070). BW turns right, but go left ('Black head Loop' fingerpost; PA) for ½ mile along lane, over stile, past house (PA). Right up path (188078), levelling out on Poulanegh Hill and turning west, following PAs to meet cobbled path (197066) after 2 miles. Downhill towards sea; left (189097) along slopes. At gate on right, keep ahead (PA) along jungly mile; descend above Aghaglinny North on to track; left along cliffs for 3¾ miles to R477; left (*take care!*) to car park.

LENGTH: 12 miles: allow 6–8 hours.

GRADE: Moderate (occasionally difficult)

CONDITIONS: Uneven stones underfoot on Poulanegh Hill; jungly stretch, slippery descent to Aghaglinny North.

DON'T MISS:
fabulous wild flowers on all sides
wild goats (keep your eyes peeled!)
Mass house and shebeen in Cathair an Aird Rois

REFRESHMENTS: None en route – take a picnic.

INFORMATION:

Tourist Office: Village Stores, Main Street, Ballyvaughan (065-707-7077); www.clare. ie; www.discoverireland.ie/destinations.

Burren Guided Walks and Hikes with Mary Howard (065-707-6100/ 087-244-6807; www.burrenguidedwalks.com).

24

WESTQUARTER, INISHBOFIN, CO GALWAY

THE LONG BLACK CURRACHS strained at their buoys in Inishbofin harbour, their retroussé noses snubbing the lines as a stiff west wind blew in from the Atlantic. A saucy cockerel screeched defiantly from his gatepost lookout, and purple orchids trembled in the breeze along the verges of the lane. Grey or fine, windy or still, Connemara exerts magic on its visitors, especially out in these humpy granite islands of the west. We were lucky to be walking Inishbofin with Gerry McCloskey, a man who has forgotten more about the islands than I've ever imagined learning.

The bare soil of Connemara's island fields has always needed to be painstakingly manured, cultivated and carefully preserved from blowing away. We passed a neat and tiny vegetable garden, the heaped ridges growing carrots, onions, lettuces, beetroot, spuds, all buttressed from the salt sea wind by sturdy stone walls. Out along the grassy track to the townland of Westquarter, the fields tended by former generations lay thick on either hand, corduroy ridges combed in parallel lines down slopes too steep and awkward for any horse plough.

Inishbofin is an island that holds its history close to the surface, to be read by anyone with a pair of eyes and a little curiosity. This rollercoaster of a track, leading out to the islanders' turf banks at the west end of Inishbofin, was built by hungry men and women as a famine road when all their sweat and labour at the potato beds turned futile overnight. There was fish, of course, but the sea was hungry, too, and it never lost its propensity to swallow men and currachs. The cliffs of Westquarter hold poignant memorials – a striking skeletal cross to Edward Moll and Richard Mathes, two Kansas students drowned while swimming, and above the beautiful creamy sands of Trá Gheal a memorial to three boys of the Lacey family, brothers Michael and Martin and their cousin Peter. All three were lost in 1949 when their currach tipped over on Easter Sunday morning as they rowed from their native Inishark to attend Mass on Inishbofin.

Inishark had no priest. The island lacked a doctor, too, and a decent harbour. When a young man died of appendicitis because help could not be fetched in time, it spelled the end for human life on Inishark. Looking across the quiet sands and the restless waters of Ship Sound to the roofless ruins of Inishark's village, imagination saw the final exodus by boat of the remaining couple of dozen islanders in 1960. They went to houses and land in Claddaghduff; their homeland entered a long isolation, still unbroken.

We turned down along crags of red shaly rock, moving across slopes where brisk little birds went skimming away, flashing their snowy rumps. They were wheatears, a politer bird-fancier's version of the earthy old name that countrymen knew them by – 'white-arse'.

The massive stone blocks of Dún Mór promontory fort clung to a green, upslanted tongue of cliff. Beyond, Gerry showed us the scoop of ground where IRA men on the run would hide from soldiers searching the island during the War of Independence. Here lies a rough and stony region, exactly resembling a beach of shingle pebbles. That's just what it was, confirmed Gerry, a raised beach, left high and dry after the Ice Age glaciers melted. All that weight of ice was lifted, and

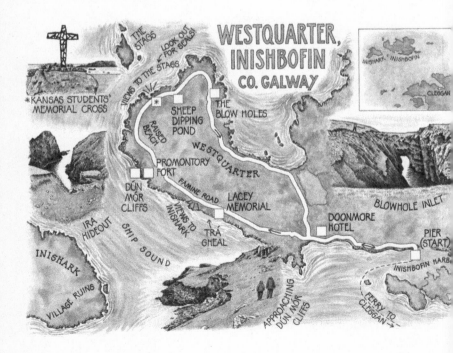

the land rose up like a sponge that had been squashed under a giant foot.

The Kansas students' memorial cross looks north towards the islets of The Stags. This is the westernmost and remotest quarter of Inishbofin, seething with the wildly tossing heads of bog cotton. We walked on, circling round the cliffs. Two enormous blowholes opened at our feet, each big enough to sink a ship in, connected by a passageway through the canted rock strata that opened to the sea. In a northerly gale the holes spew spray with a boom to frighten the devil. But today they lay quiet, in harmony with the mood of this soft grey afternoon on the western threshold of Ireland.

WAY TO GO

MAP: OS of Ireland 1:50,000 Discovery 37; downloadable map/instructions (highly recommended) at www.discoverireland.ie/walking; map-guide available on Inishbofin.

TRAVEL:

Bus (www.michaelneecoaches.com; www.citylink.ie): Galway–Cleggan.

Road: Cleggan is signed from N59 between Letterfrack and Clifden.

Ferries: Island Discovery (095-45819/45894; www.inishbofinislanddiscovery.com), King Ferries (095-44649) from Cleggan to Inishbofin.

WALK DIRECTIONS: Bear left from pier along road past Doonmore Hotel; where tarmac ends, follow famine road and waymarked paths clockwise around cliffs. At sheep-dipping pond (beyond memorial cross to Kansas students) waymarks run out; aim for skyline near coast to continue, following coast back to hotel and pier.

LENGTH: 5 miles: allow 3 hours.

GRADE: Moderate

Cont.

CONDITIONS: Grass paths; one or two slopes; can be slippery after rain. Buggy-friendly along roads. NB Cliff edges are unguarded and sheer – please take great care, especially with children and dogs.

DON'T MISS:
- views over Trá Gheal to Inishark
- Kansas students' memorial cross
- the blowholes

REFRESHMENTS/ACCOMMODATION: Doonmore Hotel (095-45814/04; www.doonmorehotel.com); Day's Hotel (095-45809; www.dayshotel.ie); Dolphin Hotel & Restaurant (095-45991; www.dolphinhotel.ie); Galley B&B and Restaurant (095-45894); Lapwing House (095-45996).

INFORMATION:

www.inishbofin.com.

Guide books/leaflets: Map-guide widely available on Inishbofin.

Connemara Safari Walking Holidays: Gerry McCloskey 095-21071 or Freephone 1850 777 200; www.walkingconnemara.com.

25
Trá Mhóir and Bunowen, Ballyconneely, Co Galway

WILD FLOWERS THICKLY STREWN across low green cliffs, larks in full song suspended on invisible wires over my head, and a blue summer sky above the Errismore peninsula of westernmost Connemara. If I'd gone any further west, I'd have been on my way to America. But who'd want any such thing on an afternoon like this?

Down below the golf links where the sward met the sand, a herd of brown and cream cattle moved with fantastic deliberation, contentedly munching a salad of grass, orchids and seaweed. No need to add salt to the butter hereabouts. Their hooves left deer-like slots in the pure white shell-sand. The rocks lay blackened with algae, patched orange with lichens. When the Connemara sun shines like this, it passes everything through a colour filter of psychedelic intensity. Great tuffets of pink sea thrift sifted the afternoon breeze, the big powder-blue blooms of sea holly rose from prickly collars of leaves, and the white sand under the waves gave the shallows a hue of jade green that the most brazen swimming pool manufacturer would blush to use.

I walked the strand of Trá Mhóir and the headlands beyond, looking out to a jigsaw of dark rocks and islets. Herring gulls skimmed the sea with creaky cries. A woman was hanging out her washing behind her white cottage, which looked out from its knoll over a pitch-encrusted pier and three red and blue trawlers. There was a masterpiece right there, just waiting for an Impressionist to slouch by.

Crunching over carpets of sun-dried kelp as black and crisp as fried onions, I came to Bunowen Pier. A seductive smell of smoked fish and tarry rope hung round the Connemara Smokehouse. I'd put a bun in my pocket before setting out, in hopes of finding their door open. Resistance was useless. Smoked tuna and brown bread, eaten on the pier with legs a-dangling and a sight of the basalt plug of Doon Hill across the crescent of Bunowen Bay. You couldn't beat that.

Up and on along the road, with the castellations and blank windows of Bunowen Castle rising under Doon Hill like something belonging to the Hammer House of Horror. The castle began life as an O'Flaherty stronghold, the most westerly one they possessed. In the 1550s it was the trading and freebooting base of the young Granuaile and her first husband Dónal an-Chogaidh O'Flaherty. In the 19th century John Augustus O'Neill bankrupted himself turning the old house into a Gothic fantasy, and it's been a ruin now for the past 100 years.

Opposite the castle lay Lough Caffrey, riffled by catspaws of wind. The claw-shaped lough has a great story attached, told by Tim Robinson in his admirable Connemara gazetteer. After a massacre of the Conneelys of Ballyconneely by the O'Flahertys, the son of the sole survivor returned to wreak revenge at a time when An Bi[o]ránach, the O'Flaherty chief, was living on a tiny islet in Lough Caffrey. Young Conneely (having first prudently practised his long-jumping) sprang from the shore on to the island in one tremendous leap, killed An Bi oránach, and reinforced his triumph by marrying O'Flaherty's daughter. Ruthlessness, athleticism, murder and romance: the absolute cornerstones of Irish myth.

I passed the skeleton of the old factory where alginic acid was once processed from seaweed for the manufacture of (among other items) toothpaste and ice-cream. Side roads snake among widely scattered houses in the low rocky landscape of Errismore. I followed them between boglands bright with yellow flags. In the tiny irregularly shaped pastures the ruins of houses crumbled and the stone walls let the sky through in shards of blue and white. A pure white mare came to show her nose over the wall, and her suede-brown foal put his silky muzzle up to be stroked.

Round the next bend I came on a Connemara roadblock. Half a dozen burly cows and their calves were munching their way up the boreen, an inch at a time. I was happy enough to sit on the wall and wait in the evening sun and wind for them to pass.

TO CLIFDEN ↗

R341

BALLYCONNEELY

EMLAGHARAN BOREEN

DUNLOUGHAN ROAD

SEAWEED FACTORY (DISUSED)

CONNEMARA GOLF CLUB CLUBHOUSE (START)

BUNOWEN CASTLE

SUPERB PROSPECT OF DOON HILL & BUNOWEN CASTLE

LOUGH CAFFREY

DOON HILL

SHORT CUT

TRÁ MHÓIR

BUNOWEN CASTLE

CONNEMARA SMOKEHOUSE

BUNOWEN BAY

FABULOUS VIEWS OVER BUNOWEN BAY

BUNOWEN PIER

SEA THRIFT AT TRÁ MHÓIR

TRÁ MHÓIR & BUNOWEN
BALLYCONNEELY, CO. GALWAY

PANORAMA OF BUNOWEN BAY & DOON HILL

WAY TO GO

MAP: OS of Ireland 1:50,000 Discovery 44; Folding Landscape map 'Connemara' (see below).

TRAVEL:

Bus (www.buseireann.ie): 419 (Clifden–Galway) to Ballyconneely (3½ miles).

Road: N59 to Clifden, R341 to Ballyconneely, right at Keogh's pub to Bunowen; right ('Connemara Golf Club') to club house. Walkers welcome to park; it's appreciated if you give the bar your custom!

WALK DIRECTIONS: Walk down golf club drive. At gate, bear right to shore. Left along strands and round headlands for 2 miles to Connemara Smokehouse at Bunowen Quay. Left up road (*short cut: in ¾ mile, left along golf course road*) for 1 mile to pass old seaweed factory on left; in 200 m, left ('Dunloughan Road' on slate in wall). In ¾ mile, left along boreen ('Emlagharan') for 1¾ miles to reach golf course road. Right to club house.

LENGTH: 7 miles (*short cut 4 miles*): allow 3 (2) hours.

GRADE: Easy

CONDITIONS: Strands, coastal rocks, grass, country roads. Buggy-friendly except along shore.

DON'T MISS:
  seaweed-munching cows
  Connemara Smokehouse
  Bunowen Castle

REFRESHMENTS: Connemara Golf Club, Bunowen (095-23502/23602; www.connemaragolflinks.com); Connemara Smokehouse (www.smokehouse.ie).

INFORMATION:

Clifden Tourist Office: 095-21163; www.connemara.ie; www.discoverireland.ie/west.

Connemara: Map and Gazetteer by Tim Robinson (Folding Landscapes, Roundstone; www.foldinglandscapes.com) is packed with fascinating information.

26

DIAMOND HILL, CONNEMARA NATIONAL PARK, CO GALWAY

DIAMOND HILL IS, FIRST and last, a proper mountain. It is easy to think of it as a tame lump, scarcely worth the attention of a proper walker. I've got to admit that that's exactly what I pictured when I heard about its neatly waymarked trails, its convenient proximity to the Connemara National Park Visitor Centre, its suitability for all ages and stages (suitably fit and equipped). Lord forgive me for my snobbery. Now I've climbed Diamond Hill, I respect it as a real Connemara mountain. It might not be one of the true apostles, the Twelve Bens themselves; but at 1,460 feet (445 metres) of climb from sea level it's a really good challenge for non-mountaineers – a true people's mountain, Everyman's Peak.

What you see from the Visitor Centre is a shapely cone, high against the eastern sky, diamond-shaped. On this bright morning it glittered like a diamond, too, as the west Galway sunshine reflected off the polished quartzite that forms the mountain. I grabbed a leaflet showing the panorama on view from the peak, and made off up the trail through birch scrub and boggy grassland trickling with yesterday's rain.

The path steepened through a wide bogland full of milky pale marsh orchids and pink fairy bonnets of lousewort, to reach a monolithic stone at the halfway point. Here was the place to halt and take in the really stupendous view back over Barnaderg Bay and Ballynakill Harbour, the sea-beast profiles of Inishbofin and Inishark out beyond the jaws of the inlet. Tully Mountain loomed dome-shaped over the harbour, and to the north Kylemore Lough stretched away toward the blunt wall of the Maumturk Mountains.

From here the blue trail fell away towards the valley, and the red Upper Diamond trail, very well engineered and drained, forged on upwards alone. Now the cone shape of the mountain changed to a long knobbly spine upheld against the clouds. Streamlets chinked and trickled unseen. A scattered chain of climbers ascended the path – French, German, American, Japanese, Danish and, yes, Irish too. A tiny tot in pink trainers went staggering up behind her big sister, all of six years old and very keen to scamper straight to the top. Mum puffed hard in the rear and called unavailingly for a little breather. Some silver scramblers overtook me, striding along. It was good to be climbing the mountain in such varied company, everyone armed with a greeting or a wry comment.

The path steepened further, zigzagging up through the rough quartzite. Feral goats surveyed the rabble with utter indifference from precarious perches on the edge of the mountain. Up at the top, jolly parties gathered round the big cairn to add a pebble and pat each other on the back. Now we could see east into the heart of the Twelve Bens, a dun and olive semi-circle of peaks and ridges, like a wire bent into sharp undulations under an army blanket.

The downward path led back to the halfway stone, then on down through sphagnum bog and a valley of flowering gorse and rowan trees. When I looked up, I saw that the mountain had shifted shape once more, the monster spine reverting to the handsome gleaming cone I'd admired at the start of the day.

The Gazetteer that accompanies Tim Robinson's definitive 'Folding Landscape' map of Connemara has an elliptical entry on Diamond Hill. 'It was said,' remarks Robinson in his dry way, 'that the poet Mac Suibhne would have climbed it had there been a tavern on top.' By all accounts Míchál Mac Suibhne was fond of the odd glass, and of pretty girls too. It's a shame he never made it to the top of Diamond Hill. He could well have found one, if not the other, up there; and the view from the summit would inspire a log of wood to verse, let alone a poet like Mac Suibhne. What a treasure he might have bequeathed us.

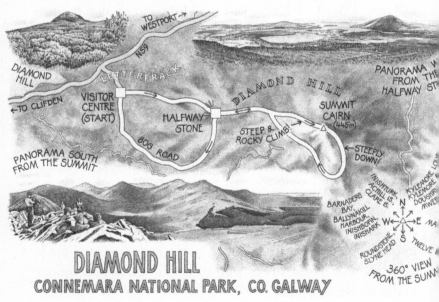

DIAMOND HILL
CONNEMARA NATIONAL PARK, CO. GALWAY

WAY TO GO

MAP: OS of Ireland 1:50,000 Discovery 37; Folding Landscapes map and gazetteer Connemara' (www.foldinglandscapes.com); downloadable map/instructions (highly recommended) at www.discoverireland.ie/walking.

TRAVEL:

Bus (www.buseireann.ie) to Letterfrack: 419 Galway–Clifden, 421 Galway–Westport.

Road: Connemara National Park Centre is signposted off N59 Clifden–Leenane road in Letterfrack.

WALK DIRECTIONS: 4 trails available, in order of difficulty: Ellis Wood (½ mile, green waymarks), Sruffaunboy (1 mile, yellow waymarks), Lower Diamond Hill (2 miles, blue waymarks, Upper Diamond Hill (2¼ miles, red). Pick and mix as you prefer. The walk described follows Upper Diamond Hill from Visitor Centre to the summit and back to the Big Stone. Left here on the Bog Trail, back to Visitor Centre.

LENGTH: 4¼ miles: allow 2–3 hours.

GRADE: Hard

CONDITIONS: Good path, duckboards or steps underfoot; many stone drainage gullies, so watch your step! Upper Diamond Hill a steep, rough ascent, but active children, properly shod, can make it to the top. Take raingear, a snack and drink – it's a proper mountain. Avoid upper section in heavy rain/mist/high wind.

DON'T MISS:

Connemara National Park Visitor Centre

wild goats – keep your eyes peeled!

fabulous 360° views from summit

REFRESHMENTS: Visitor Centre.

INFORMATION:

Connemara National Park Visitor Centre: Letterfrack; 095-41054/41006; www.connemaranationalpark.ie.

Diamond Hill Panorama leaflet from Connemara National Park Visitor Centre.

27

CHILDREN OF LIR LOOP, CARROWTEIGE, CO MAYO

IT WAS A COLD windy morning over north-west Mayo, with just enough blue in the sky to make a pair of Dutchman's trousers. Or a pair of Mayoman's longjohns, come to that – there were enough of them on display around Carrowteige, cheerfully flapping on washing lines in the brisk spring wind as if waving goodbye to winter.

Carrowteige is one of Mayo's remotest Gaeltacht outposts, a scattered village hidden in a vast landscape of bog and windswept mountainside. I was delighted to meet Treasa Ní Ghearraigh and her husband Uinsíonn Mac Graith in the Seanscoil community centre. The Children of Lir Loop Walk around the spectacular cliffs near Benwee Head is one of the local walks projects which Treasa and Uinsíonn have helped create as a labour of love for their native corner of the world. 'Never spoke a word of English till I went to school,' declared Uinsíonn as he and fellow walker Pádraig O Dochartaigh accompanied me down the shore road. 'And I wouldn't speak it even now among family and friends.'

The mound that holds the remnants of the church of St Ghallagáin dominates its lonely shoreline graveyard. Local people had the custom of burying their dead as close to the mound as possible, and so the graveyard came into being, an egalitarian resting place for Catholics, Protestants, unbaptised babes and nameless drowned sailors washed up by the tides. Climbing the mound, Uinsíonn turned over a long slab of stone and rubbed a wisp of grass along its surface. As if by magic, the outline of a Maltese cross appeared. 'Early Christian,' murmured Uinsíonn. 'Well, we'll leave you to your walk now – I don't think you'll be disappointed.'

That was the understatement of the century. What unrolled over the next couple of hours was one of the most breathtakingly wild and beautiful coastal walks I've ever encountered. At hand all the way as a reliable guide was the stumpy sod fence of the Black Ditch, a half-toppled wall built and repaired over the centuries to stop cattle and sheep tumbling over the cliffs. Crossing its course lay long parallel lines of potato ridges, the very stamp and symbol of the Great Hunger that still scars all these western landscapes. I stood by the Black Ditch, the wind smacking at my face, looking down to Tráigh na bhFothantaí Dubha, the beach of the black precipices, where the sea creamed in tight ruffs of white foam under dark cliffs.

Following the Black Ditch up on to the crest of the mountain, I was hit with another, even more jaw-dropping prospect – a landward view filled with immensities of bog seamed with the black lines of turf banks, a seaward panorama of great stepped cliff edges full of huge dark hollows, rising to the magnificent 830-foot prow of Benwee Head. Just offshore, Kid Island rose from a collar of spume. The sight of  its fierce cliffs, and the tiny white dots of sheep along its green back, prompted two thoughts – just how in heaven did they get up there, and just how the hell would the farmer gather them again?

A few steps more and I was gazing out at the Stags of Broadhaven, five sharply cut shark teeth of rock rearing out of the sea a couple of miles off Benwee Head. This is a landscape in which one can believe anything might happen – even the salvation of four suffering exiles transformed by sorcery into swans. It was out on Inisglora, hidden away on the far side of the Mullet peninsula, that the Children of Lir eventually found burial and absolution. But it's on the cliffs just north of Carrowteige that a modern sculpture has been erected in their honour.

I wouldn't be bold enough to attempt an artistic critique of this assemblage of pipes, tubes and stonework. But everything has its uses, doesn't it? I found, to my pleasure, that the pipes had been tuned to the key of G, and had fun knocking 'Lanigan's Ball' out of them with my walking stick.

BENWEE HEAD & STAGS OF BROADHAVEN

CLIFFS SOUTH OF KID ISLAND

SHEEP ROAD BLOCK!

KID ISLAND

HOW DID THE SHEEP GET UP HERE??

FAB VIEWS

CHILDREN OF LIR MONUMENT

ART & MUSIC IN ONE!

GET YOUR PICNIC HERE

CARROWTEIGE

GARVIN'S SHOP

SHORT STEEP PUFF UPHILL

TO BALLYCASTLE

BLACK DITCH

SEANSCOIL CENTRE (START & FINISH)

SUPERB VIEWS SOUTH OVER THE BAYS

POTATO RIDGES

CILL Á GHALLAGÁIN GRAVEYARD

TRÁIGH NA BHFOTHANTAÍ DUBHA

TRÁIGH A' PHOIRT

UINSÍONN ON ST. GHALLAGÁIN'S MOUND

BINROE POINT

CHILDREN OF LIR LOOP, CARROWTEIGE CO. MAYO

POTATO RIDGES & THE VIEW SOUTH

WAY TO GO

MAP: OS of Ireland 1:50,000 Discovery 22; downloadable map/instructions at www discoverireland.ie/walking.

TRAVEL:

Road: R314/315 to Ballycastle; R314 to Belderg, minor roads via Porturlin and Portacloy to Carrowteige.

WALK DIRECTIONS: (blue arrows/BA): Leaving the Seanscoil, right up road; in 200 m, fork left (BA) on road past Cill á Ghallagáin graveyard. Continue down to shore; right up tarmac road (BA) for 400 m, then left across machair, to follow Black Ditch sod fence along cliffs (take care!) for 2 miles (BA) to reach Children of Lir (BA) monument. Inland (BA) along road. In ½ mile, just after bog road joins on right, turn left (BA) on road to Carrowteige.

LENGTH: 6½ miles: allow 2½–3 hours.

GRADE: Moderate/Hard

CONDITIONS: Boggy along Black Ditch – wear boots! A couple of steep, short climbs/descents. Cliff edge unfenced: keep dogs and kids under strict control.

DON'T MISS:
- view over Tráigh na bhFothantaí Dubha from Black Ditch path
- view of Stags of Broadhaven from cliffs near monument
- Children of Lir monument

REFRESHMENTS: None en route; picnic from Garvin's shop, Carrowteige.

INFORMATION:

Tourist Office: James Street, Westport; 098-25711; www.discoverireland.ie/west.

The Placenames and Heritage of Dún Chaocháin by Uinsíonn Mac Graith and Treas Ní Ghearraigh, and other booklets, etc., available at the Seanscoil, Carrowteige (097 88082; dunchaochain1@eircom.net).

28

CLOGHER BOG,
CO MAYO

THE NEW-BORN LAMBS IN the townland of Newtown hadn't yet grown into their wrinkly skins, which hung on them like poorly fitting home-knit sweaters. They needed their natural pullovers, too, on this sunny spring afternoon with a brisk north wind streaming across the Plains of Mayo. Jane and I smacked our gloved hands together as we set out from Clogher Heritage Centre, a working forge and a thatched cottage complete with butter churns, a proper old 'hag's bed' and a cheerful fire. The cottage forms the hub of the Clogher Bog Looped Walk, a superb circular route through some of rural Mayo's most characteristic country.

Our companions on this blowy afternoon were Anna Connor, who has been establishing new walking routes all across Mayo, and local woman-of-knowledge Mary McDonagh. 'I work at training unemployed people,' Mary explained, 'and they helped the community of Clogher to develop the Heritage Centre. But then we thought: well, that's great, but how do we attract people to come and see it? That's how the bog walk started.'

Anyone who loves and appreciates bogland doesn't need to be told of this environment's subtle beauty and endless variety. But many still discount the bog as a waste of space, ugly and empty. Here's the walk to change their minds for them.

Down in the south-west the ice-blue ridges of the Partry Mountains humped up on the flat horizon under a streaky sky – perfect targets for a well-aimed telephoto lens. Songbirds fluted from the silver birch scrub as we tramped a bog road through heather burned by a recent fire to charcoal black and brilliant orange. 'Only a month ago people were skating on the floods out here,' noted Mary. 'A bog's well able to cope with these big changes.'

Two bog horses approached out of the gorse, but their palates were too fine for the whisp of grass I held out. They sniffed it, then drew back their dark lips and snorted in disapproval. We had better luck with the old donkey at Doonamon; he put his nose over the fence to be stroked, and nodded vigorously as though to say: 'OK, but where's the sugar lump?'

By the ancient ring forts of Fortlawn and Lissalackaun a massively thick wall crossed the fields. Built by a farmer, Mary said, from the stones of some ancient houses he'd knocked. And the names of the families who'd lived there? 'Morning, Noone and Knight,' she recounted, 'Rabbitte, Fox and Hare! Strange, but true!'

Information notices fixed to trees along the Clogher Bog walk give fascinating snippets of folklore. Alder's unlucky; a hazelnut in your pocket guards against the rheumatics; whitethorn's a fairy tree that can harm those rash enough to abuse it. Not so long ago every country man and woman knew these things, but not in this scientific and rational generation.

'An rud is annamh is iontach,' said the notice by an old thorn tree – 'Whatever is strange is wonderful.'

Strange and wonderful is the long slim footprint of St Patrick blazoned on a rock beyond Drom cemetery. It looks as though the saint took a size 16 sandal, at least – just one more enticing oddity of this stroll through an unregarded landscape.

'The number of people going out walking has taken a huge step up lately,' observed Anna as we headed for home, 'but it's hard to say exactly why.' Mary stopped and looked reflectively around over bog, scrub and iridescent pools. 'I'd say in the hard old days everyone was out working the land all the time, so they didn't want to walk it for pleasure. But now you'll see people out doing this walk after they've driven home from work – they just enjoy the land, without associating it with all that hard labour and those hard times.'

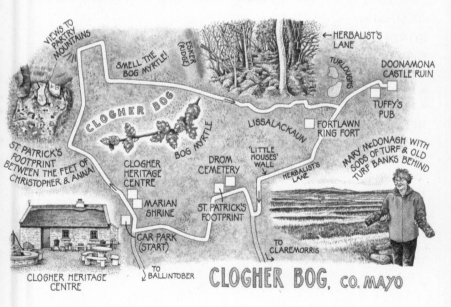

CLOGHER HERITAGE CENTRE

CLOGHER BOG, CO. MAYO

145

WAY TO GO

MAP: OS of Ireland 1:50,000 Discovery 31,38; downloadable map/instructions (highly recommended) at www.discoverireland.ie/walking.

TRAVEL:

Rail (www.irishrail.ie): Manulla Junction (6 miles).

Road: Clogher is signed off N84 Ballinrobe–Castlebar near Ballintober.

WALK DIRECTIONS: Take left fork at Marian shrine beside Clogher Heritage Centre. Follow purple arrows (PA) up road for ⅔ mile; then right on to bog road (PA). Follow PAs through twists and turns across Clogher Bog, then east along road past Doonamona to T-junction beside lakes. Turn left for ¼ mile to Tuffy's pub opposite Doonamona Castle ruin; then return to lake junction and continue Looped Walk route along road. In ¼ mile, right through stile (this is a section of Croagh Patrick Heritage Trail, with yellow 'walking man' waymarks). Follow these plus PAs, aiming half right across field; cross stile (PA); follow PAs by wall and on for ½ mile to cross road and pass Drom Cemetery and St Patrick's footprint. Over boggy fields; left along lane; return to Clogher Heritage Centre.

LENGTH: 5½ miles: allow 2–3 hours.

GRADE: Easy

CONDITIONS: Bog roads, tarmac roads, muddy field paths.

DON'T MISS:
- Clogher Heritage Centre (http://www.museumsofmayo.com/clogher.htm)
- beautiful scent of bog myrtle (pinch it and sniff!)
- St Patrick's footprint

REFRESHMENTS: Tuffy's pub, Doonamona (24 hrs notice, please, for soup/sandwich lunch – 087-756-0435).

ACCOMMODATION: McWilliam Park Hotel, Claremorris; 094-937-8000; www.mcwilliamparkhotel.ie.

INFORMATION:

Tourist Office: Linenhall Street, Castlebar; 094-902-1207; www.discoverireland.ie/west.

29

DERRYLAHAN LOOP, CLOONFAD, CO ROSCOMMON

'*CLOONFAD? OH, THE BACK* blocks!'

'Aye, they lost a couple of fellows in there last year – neither hide nor hair of 'em seen since.'

The jolly drinkers in Roscommon's Abbey Hotel were getting great gas out of the thought of me venturing into the southwest tip of the county. The way they talked it up, I'd need an elephant gun and a pocketful of quinine just to survive. Myself, I could hardly wait. Roscommon is one of those edge-of-the-Midlands counties it's all too easy to sidle by on your way to the grandeurs of the west. But I'd noticed enough bird-haunted forest and sunsplashed bog on previous glancing contacts with the place to have promised myself to come back with my boots on one day.

On a morning cold enough to nip the fingers, with a muted pearly light overhead and in among the conifers, I found my way to Derrylahan Resource Centre. Beside the building stood a tiny domed structure of stone – an ancient sweathouse, recently restored. You'd need to be extremely thin, or to be given a cruel kicking as incentive, to force your way inside that diminutive bee-hive hut. Once there, you'd be baked alive till the sickness was out of you, then extracted and chucked in an ice-cold stream. It was kill or cure in the old days: no namby-pambies survived around Derrylahan.

The bluish bottle-brush sprouts of the sitka spruce in Derrylahan Forest made a sombre backdrop for the tender green leaves breaking out on willows, hazels and birches all around. A robin sat on the topmost branch of a pine tree and sang as if about to burst with glee. Bog ditches glinted iridescent and thick in the strengthening sunshine. Even the darkly mysterious realm under the conifers, so redolent of Grimm fairy tales, of horrid stepmothers and cannibalistic witches, seemed exorcised by spring.

Derrylahan hamlet lay among the daffodils – a neat white dwelling next to a tumbledown older neighbour in a hollow of dog's mercury and moss. The world seemed out on its doorstep today. In nearby Cloonerkaun an old man in billycock hat and paint-splashed overalls was so busy whitewashing the stains of winter from his barn that he didn't even look up as I went whistling by.

The advance of Derrylahan Forest has captured several townlands and their small farms whose walled fields lay wholly overgrown with stiffly rustling clumps of rushes. Beyond Cloonerkaun, though, the trees stepped back and a long and wide bog landscape unrolled northwards. Some patches bristled with the wind-bleached bones of old trees; others lay littered with coarse grey rocks studded with jewel-like blobs of gleaming white quartzite. In there somewhere, according to the map, a Mass Rock and a cillín were to be found. I scoured the dun and ochre landscape with binoculars, but never spotted them. It didn't matter – I was contented to leave them in silent concealment, and to stroll on across the bog with lark song and wind whistle for company.

The sun released rich smells from the bog: heather, dry grasses and wet turf, myrtle, and something eucalyptus-like that I couldn't identify. I took a detour and found Brid Bourke's Cross, very roughly fashioned, rising from a haphazard grave of stone slabs. 'RIP Brid Bourke, Drumbane' was the simple inscription lettered in trickly black paint on the cross. Who was Brid Bourke? There were no clues. And where was the standing stone the map showed at the crest of Slieve Dart? I didn't find it when I climbed there for the wind and the 50-mile view towards Connemara. I couldn't have cared less. The back blocks of south-west Roscommon get you right in the heart, with all their mysteries and subtle beauty. Who'd want to be anywhere else on a spring day such as this?

WAY TO GO

MAP: OS of Ireland 1:50,000 Discovery 39; downloadable map/instructions at www. discoverireland.ie/walking.

TRAVEL:

Rail (www.irishrail.ie) or bus (www.buseireann.ie) to Ballyhaunis (5 miles from Cloonfad).

Road: Follow 'Scenic Walk Resource Centre' sign from R327 Williamstown road, 2 miles east of Cloonfad.

WALK DIRECTIONS: (purple arrow/PA waymarks): Leaving Resource Centre (OS ref M 536695), turn right along road, round sharp left bend; first left (PA) past Derrylahan hamlet for 1 mile to road at Cloonerkaun. Turn right; ignore 'Scenic Walk' sign on left and continue along road for ½ mile. Beyond farm on left, bear left on green track, SW, for ⅓ mile to a step-over stile (M 522700 approx – NB: waymarks briefly disappear here). Cross stile, then another lower down (522698). Keep ahead with drain on your left to road (waymarks resume). Forward for 50 m; forward at left bend (PA) on bog road. Follow PAs for ½ mile to forest road (516689). Left for 1½ miles to Resource Centre.

Detours: (a) left at 522689 to Brid Bourke's Cross (signed); (b) right just before Resource Centre up forest road to viewpoint on Slieve Dart.

LENGTH: 5 miles: allow 3 hours.

GRADE: Easy

CONDITIONS: Forest roads and tracks, bog paths. Two step-over stiles.

DON'T MISS:
- the rich smell of the bog in sunshine
- Brid Bourke's Cross
- view from Slieve Dart

REFRESHMENTS: Take a picnic – several tables along walk.

INFORMATION:

Roscommon Tourist Office: 090-66-26342; www.discoverireland.ie/west.

Guide books/leaflets: From Derrylahan Resource Centre (contact Cloonfad Scenic Walks, 087-239-6985).

30

ARIGNA MINER'S WAY, CO ROSCOMMON

A CRISP DAY AFTER rain, with streaks of cloud over Lough Allen and the Iron Mountains. A sharp wind blew from Leitrim into Roscommon, streaming the smoke from the chimney at Arigna Fuels into long tatters, soon snatched away. I climbed the long lane from Derreenavoggy Bridge towards Kilronan Mountain, hunched far into my coat collar. Two ladies came down the road, each bearing a bucket brimming with clear spring water. 'Oh, we've tap water in the house, all right,' they chirruped, 'but 'tis only for the washing. We'd never make the tea or boil the vegetables without the good water from the spring well!'

The lane levelled out and snaked along the hillside. Glancing over a gate, I made out a couple of shadowy stone chambers side by side under a bank, half smothered in ferns. Sweathouses! Good Lord, what our ancestors put up with before the advent of modern medicine. Why the country round Lough Allen should have been so well stocked with sweathouses, no one seems to know. Sufferers from a broad range of maladies from fevers and headaches to rheumatics and madness were stripped and inserted into these tiny stone hutches, to

cook and sweat in the roaring heat of a turf fire. Then they were pulled out and pushed into a freezing cold plunge tub – a primitive form of sauna treatment.

I left the lane and climbed a steep path of mud and stones to where another sweathouse loomed out of a bank. From here green field paths and stony moorland tracks led me over moorland under a great round cairn topped with a beehive of stones at the ridge of Kilronan Mountain. A stop, a sit-down and a chance to gasp at the five-star view over Lough Allen and the twin lakes of Meelagh and Skean, with the long whaleback of Sliabh an Iarainn beyond, the highest point of the Iron Mountains where iron ore was once extensively mined. But it was another kind of mineral entirely that made the name and fame of Arigna.

Soon the blackened heaps of coal mining spoil began to lump up beside the path. I snaked around between them, then plunged down the hillside to follow a lane to the extraordinary, futuristic buildings of the Arigna Mining Experience, canted at 45° and apparently sliding sideways into the ground.

Many a former industry has rebranded its leisure-orientated ghost an 'Experience'. But the Arigna mine tour truly earns that title. From a superb display of photographs of grubby-faced miners I entered the mine itself in the company of Michael, a wonderfully humorous man with 30 years at the coal face behind him. 'Riddled with tunnels, the Arigna mine,' he intoned, his voice echoing back from the rough-hewn walls. 'A wet mine, too. We'd see stalactites of iron forming on the tunnel roof. Soda bread and cold sweet tea, that was it. You'd to lie on your side to pick and shovel the coal.'

We tramped the eerie tunnels, hefted the solid weight of pickaxes and pneumatic drills, and marvelled at the vast 'Iron Man' coal cutting machine that rendered both of the hand-wielded tools redundant. Back out in the sweet rainy air of Roscommon, everything smelt wonderful. Down in the Miner's Bar by Derreenavoggy Bridge I stood with a pint of Guinness, looking at a display of mining memorabilia – helmets, lamps, tokens, photos of tired, black-faced men. Michael's parting shot ran through my head: 'It was very hard, tiring work, aye. But there was something about it that kept you down there – kept you coming back to it. Mining got in your blood, I suppose. That was it.'

ARIGNA MINER'S WAY
CO. ROSCOMMON

KILRONAN MOUNTAIN

SPOIL HEAPS

ARIGNA MINING EXPERIENCE

A FASCINATING TOUR UNDERGROUND!

DERREENAVOGG BRIDGE

TO DRUMSHANB

MINER'S BAR (START & FINISH)

ARIGNA FUELS

MINING MEMORABILIA IN THE MINER'S BAR

Arigna River

FABULOUS VIEWS OVER LOUGH ALLEN & IRON MOUNTAINS

CAIRN

SWEATHOUSE

COTTAGES

'MINER'S WAY' MARKER ON LEFT

PAIR OF SWEATHOUSES (TINY STONE CHAMBERS IN THE BANK)

154

WAY TO GO

MAP: OS of Ireland 1:50,000 Discovery 26; also in *Miner's Way* booklet (see below).

TRAVEL:

Arigna is signposted from R280 Drumshanbo–Drumkeeran road just north of junction with R285 Keadew road, 2½ miles from Drumshanbo.

WALK DIRECTIONS: From Miner's Bar at Derreenavoggy Bridge (OSI ref 193314), uphill. Just past Arigna Fuels, keep ahead up lane; in 300 m, over crossroads, on uphill. In ½ mile pass cottages on right, then lane; in 250 m, sweathouses over gate on right. In another 200 m, 'Miner's Way' post on left; right up steps; up path; at top, right (arrow) past another sweathouse. Follow marker posts and yellow waymarks. Left over stile on to path across moorland. In ½ mile, right (arrow) towards Lough Allen. At escarpment edge, left over stiles and through gates (arrows) for ½ mile to Miner's Way fingerpost. Don't turn downhill, but continue for ½ mile through old colliery sites, then right downhill (arrows), and right along road. In 1 mile pass Arigna Mining Experience on right; continue, and in ½ mile, left down lane to Miner's Bar.

LENGTH: 5 miles: allow 2½ hours.

GRADE: Moderate

DON'T MISS:
- the sweathouses – keep your eyes peeled!
- views from Kilronan Mountain over Lough Allen and Iron Mountains
- Arigna Mining Experience

REFRESHMENTS: Miner's Bar, Derreenavoggy Bridge (071-964-6007) – lots of mining memorabilia.

INFORMATION:

Tourist Office: Boyle (071-966-2145), Roscommon (090-662-6342) or Sligo (071-916-1201); www.discoverireland.ie/northwest.

Miner's Way & Historical Trail map guide booklet, from local tourist offices and shops, or from EastWest Mapping (053-937-7835; sales@eastwestmapping.ie).

Arigna Mining Experience: 071-964-6466; www.arignaminingexperience.ie.

31

EDENMORE BOG WALK, BALLINAMUCK, CO LONGFORD

SEAMUS TIERNEY, FRANCIS CONNELL and J.P. Sheridan were out with their shovels on Edenmore Bog this very fine morning, putting the finishing touches to the newly established bog walk. As members of RSS, the Rural Social Scheme, they're part of a team that fixes all kinds of things in the landscape of County Longford. It was Longford Community Resources Ltd, a bit of a mouthful but a long-sighted organisation, that got the Failte Ireland-sponsored looped walks off the drawing board and on to the ground locally, with the very enthusiastic help of Ballinamuck Enterprise Co-operative, based in Ballinamuck village just across the main road from the bog. It's been an exercise in co-operation, delicate at times, ultimately triumphant, bringing funding, organisation and expert local knowledge together so that walkers and birders, lovers of solitude and appreciators of the lovely and much-overlooked back country of County Longford can taste the benefit.

How many times have I sped through Longford on the great roads west to Sligo and Mayo, never even turning my head as the gentle green country slipped unemphatically by? Yet just off the highway lie landscapes of seductive subtlety: folds of farmland, drumlin ridges, unexpected lakes, and thousands of acres of bog land. Remarkable bogs! Most folk ignore them, many are repelled by their apparent lifelessness and emptiness. Exploited, battered, bruised and cut open, they are the best self-healers in nature. Birds thrive in their scrub trees, bees forage in their heathers, frogs fill their ditches with spawn. They steam richly in sunshine after rain, exuding smells as rich and sweet as new bread. And they absorb the carbon dioxide and lock in the methane that we are all learning to fear. Useful, beautiful and under-appreciated, the Irish bog is one of my favourite places on earth.

Con Halton and Dominic Halse had elected to accompany me today on the walk they'd helped create. 'The bog is such a therapeutic place,' remarked local man Maurice Murphy as he came the first step of the way with us. 'If it's been a bad day at work, you come out here for an hour's walk, and that sorts out your head for you.'

The sun streamed down out of a completely cloudless sky as we followed the grassy bog road into the wilderness. Purple moor grass bleached to pale silver tufted the bog, along with dark patches of heather. Silver birch trunks glowed in the strong sunlight, and long-tailed tits gave out their needly little songs from the scrub. I could feel the tension and pressure unpeeling, and imagined myself shedding my gnarly urban carapace and stepping out naked and open to nature.

Far out in the bog an elderly man was throwing dry sods of turf from his last year's cut into an ancient wheelbarrow, the hollow clang of the sods coming clearly in the still air. He bent and straightened with a slow, practised rhythm, the focus of a timeless tableau of manual labour under the sun.

'My father, now,' said Con Halton, as he watched the turf saver, 'he and a neighbour cut a whole winter's supply in a single day, from seven in the morning till late at night. They never broke their fast all day – and they didn't that night either, because each wife had thought the other was preparing the dinner!'

Reeks of cut turf five feet high and 50 long stood on the edge of the black cliffs of peat from which they'd been harvested. But the cut bog, after all, was only a fraction of the whole. The grass path led us on and on, through groves of black sally powdered with catkins, past birch stands hazed with green and osier clumps of pure sunlit scarlet. Larks sang their tiny heads off overhead. In the very middle of Edenmore Bog, with iridescent pools glinting far and near, we stopped to listen. Bird song; wind in the grasses; buzz of a bee; rustle of willow fronds. That was it; a place of absolute peace and quiet, with its life in proper balance.

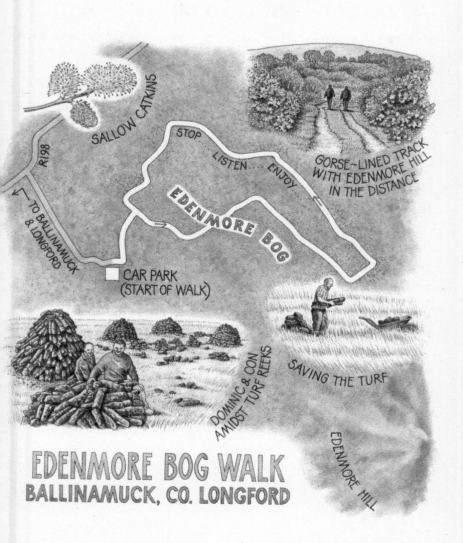

SALLOW CATKINS

R198

TO BALLINAMUCK & LONGFORD

STOP... LISTEN.... ENJOY...

EDENMORE BOG

GORSE~LINED TRACK WITH EDENMORE HILL IN THE DISTANCE

CAR PARK (START OF WALK)

DOMINIC & CON AMIDST TURF REEKS

SAVING THE TURF

EDENMORE HILL

EDENMORE BOG WALK
BALLINAMUCK, CO. LONGFORD

WAY TO GO

MAP: OS of Ireland 1:50,000 Discovery 34; downloadable map/instructions at www. discoverireland.ie/walking.

TRAVEL:

R198 Longford towards Arvagh; pass left turn to Ballinamuck; in ¾ mile, right on L 50581 ('National Looped Walk Trailhead'); in ½ mile, car park on left (OS ref N207895).

WALK DIRECTIONS: (purple arrows/p.a.): Continue down road from car park. In 20 m, left ('Edenmore Bog Walk') to T-junction of tracks; turn right and follow p.a. across bog for 1 mile to road (221895). Left (p.a.) for 150 m, left (p.a.) on bog road, following p.a., to complete anticlockwise circuit and return to car park.

LENGTH: 3½ miles: allow 2 hours.

GRADE: Easy

CONDITIONS: Good bog tracks.

DON'T MISS:
- Ballinamuck Interpretive Centre
- the chance to stand and savour the silence
- turf-cutting activities

REFRESHMENTS: The Pikeman Inn (a.k.a. Dillon's), Ballinamuck (043-332-4137) – a shrine to 1798 and good company.

INFORMATION:

Woodland & Bog Walks in County Longford, available from Ballinamuck Interpretive Centre.

Ballinamuck Interpretive Centre: open by arrangement (087-383-4706 or 043-24168); key at Pikeman Inn opposite.

32

MULLAGHMEEN FOREST, CO WESTMEATH

T HERE ARE WOODLAND WALKS so boring you think
you'll scream if you see another wretched conifer; and
then there are woodland walks like those in Mullaghmeen
Forest up in the northernmost tip of County Westmeath. The
great thing about Mullaghmeen, apart from its location as a
delightful surprise in a Midlands county not exactly celebrated
for its walking grandeurs, is its huge variety. There are certainly
sitka spruce, Scots pine and fir trees; but the 400 hectares of
Mullaghmeen, founded on fertile limestone and threaded with
waymarked trails, also contain the most extensive planted
beech forest in Ireland. That means beautiful colours in spring
and autumn, carpets of bluebells in early summer, and plenty
of dappled sunlight penetrating the leafy canopy of the wood.

A calm, cool morning, and the slender beech trunks of
Mullaghmeen Forest made a haze of pinky-grey on their hill.
Among the trees it was wonderfully quiet and peaceful, each
footfall muffled in a shroud of leaves. The hillsides were lumpy
with limestone outcrops just under a green velvet skin of moss.
We stopped on the path up through the wood to watch a
chaffinch pecking and hopping among the leaves at our feet,
quite unafraid. I thought I heard the tinkling, metallic trilling
of a wood warbler, but if so the olive and yellow songster was
keeping well out of sight.

Up on the hill a section of the forest has been planted with native Irish species, a welcome but tiny drop in the ocean of trees that the country needs. At the turn of the 20th century only 1 per cent of Ireland enjoyed tree cover; all the rest had been chopped and burned over the millennia to clear land for farming. Nowadays, thanks to the efforts of Coillte and private landowners, one hectare in ten is under trees, though not enough are natives of the kind labelled and growing here in the Mullaghmeen arboretum: whitebeam, hornbeam, wild cherry and bird cherry, whitethorn and blackthorn, crab apple and spindle, alder and elder, beautiful names with poetry running through them.

Now the path dipped to skirt the south-west margin of the wood, with views out across the undulating pastureland of Westmeath, winking with turloughs or seasonal lakes, half full after recent rain. The track sloped steeply up from Rathshane, curled aside and climbed out of the trees on to the heathery nape of Mullaghmeen Hill. Up by the summit cairn at 261 metres, we weren't exactly reaching for the oxygen and yak-skin mittens, but we were the highest creatures in low-rolling Westmeath. Were those really the Wicklow Hills, 50 miles away on the south-east skyline; the Cuilcaghs or the Iron Mountains, 40 miles off on the opposite rim of the compass? Maybe wishing made them so. But there certainly was a superb prospect of the dark waters of Lough Sheelin, spread below

with its islands and broad-headed peninsulas at the meeting point of Cavan, Meath and Westmeath.

Forests swallow ancient landscapes, as they would swallow us and all our works, given half a chance. Down below the summit, mossy humps under the beech trees showed where tiny squared-off famine fields, each carefully embanked, had been absorbed by the ever-growing wood. Up a marked side path I came to a roofless rectangle of stone, mossy and full of ferns, its back wall the rocky face of the hillside – a lonely booley hut where transhumance herdsmen lived summer-long with their cattle, making cheese and butter. Among the trees further down the hillside gleamed boggy hollows, all that remains of the retting ponds where flax was once steeped to 'ret' or rot the inner stalk away from the precious fibres used for spinning.

The poignancy of these lost working landscapes, so central to the everyday lives of our forefathers, so utterly irrelevant in the modern world, stayed in my mind for the rest of the walk, and long afterwards too.

FAMINE FIELD WALL →

FABULOUS VIEWS ALL ROUND ~A GREAT PICNIC SPOT →

SUMMIT CAIRN (261m)

BEAR LEFT AT WOODEN HUT

TURN RIGHT ON UNMARKED TRACK →

← FAMINE FIELDS

RATHSHANE

STEEP CLIMB!

BOOLEY HUT

FAMINE GARDEN

NATIVE WOODLAND ARBORETUM

FLAX PITS

VIEWS OVER WESTMEATH PASTURES & TURLOUGHS

BOOLEY HUT

CAR PARK (START)

FOREST ENTRANCE

TO CASTLEPOLLARD

ELDER

MULLAGHMEEN FOREST
CO. WESTMEATH

WAY TO GO

MAP: OS of Ireland 1:50,000 Discovery 41; downloadable map/instructions (highly recommended) at www.discoverireland.ie/walking or www.coillteoutdoors.ie.

TRAVEL:

Signposted from R394 Castlepollard–Finnea, and R154 Oldcastle-Mount Nugent.

WALK DIRECTIONS: From car park follow 'White Walk'/WW (white waymarks, white-topped posts) uphill. Detour round Native Woodland Arboretum; continue along WW. Short steep climb at Rathshane to higher path (WW and Red Walk/RW). Left along it; in 100 m pass RW turning on right ('car park'); in another 350 m, turn right up wide, unmarked track. At edge of trees keep ahead; in 100 m track curves right and climbs to summit cairn. Continue along ridge track, descending into woods and bearing right to descend to RW. Left along it for 10 m; left by hut and bench up woodland path to meet WW. Right; follow back to car park. NB – famine fields and garden off to left of WW. Booley hut detour marked on right just beyond (right up path; in 300 m, right again to hut; return to WW). Flax Pits signed off WW to right, nearer car park.

LENGTH: 6 miles: allow 2½-3 hours.

GRADE: Moderate

CONDITIONS: Well-surfaced woodland paths; good waymarking. There's a buggy/ wheelchair-friendly track from the car park to a viewing point with benches.

DON'T MISS:
- Native Woodland Arboretum
- view from summit
- famine fields

REFRESHMENTS: None en route – take a picnic.

INFORMATION:

Mullingar Tourist Office: Market Square (044-934-8650);

http://www.discoverireland.ie/eastcoast/visit/westmeath.aspx.

33

WESTMEATH WAY, NEAR MULLINGAR, CO WESTMEATH

HEAVY CLOUD MOVED ACROSS the flat lake country of Westmeath, shot through by sun and stirred by wind. Kayaks and rubber ribs lay piled against the climbing wall at the Lilliput Adventure Centre, and beyond on the shores of Lough Ennell a group of children whooped and called, delighted to be let out of the classroom to orienteer through head-high reeds and grass. The soft yellow-grey catkins of the willows were alive with bees crazy for nectar, their bumbly bodies dusted yellow with pollen grains as they staggered half-drunk from tree to tree.

Westmeath seems a county made for early summer – something about its thick black soil, somnolent cows and broad, low-lying pastures. The fields lie rumpled into ridges by the underlying gravel heaps called eskers, left behind when the glaciers packed up and went north 10,000 years ago. The Westmeath Way followed an old avenue of beech trees away from the lough, a green lane into the heart of a wide swath of bog where cattle stood chin-deep in lush grass under scrub birches loud with wrens.

Turf banks, tin turf huts, and a bog farm way out in the wild. If you were looking for a place to sit easy with sandwiches and flask, this could be the spot – or maybe a mile further along on the banks of the eel-brown Dysart River, where in a watery dell under hazel trees Jane and I found a pair of gateposts leading to a poignant group of ruins. Someone once loved and cared for this nameless farmstead, shaping the barn lintel into a pleasing bow, building a concrete porch whose front door now opens into nothing. Ivy and fern, those infinitely slow but sure invaders, are capturing the place. 'Isn't there a lovely sense of calm here?' mused Jane as she fingered the mossy stones. 'They had fuel, water, shelter – everything they needed. I wonder if they got rich enough to go off and buy a modern bungalow, and were they happier there?'

The Westmeath Way led off beside the gravel-bedded Dysart through sedgy fields where the brown water came squirting up at every step, making us thankful for gaiters and proper leather boots – not those cloth-topped nonsenses that the outdoor shops try to flog poor innocent walkers. I've tried 'em, and chucked 'em. You might as well go out shod with sponges.

At Dysart three donkeys looked over their paddock hedge, and a fierce little tyke of a dog mounted guard at his front gate with a brave show of soprano yapping. Beyond by the ruins of Dysart Church we caught a gleam of Lough Ennell, lying low at the foot of the slope. Held tight in the circle of a wildly overgrown graveyard, the ivy-smothered church stood knee-deep in bluebells. St Coleman founded a monastery here above the lake; Cromwell's men smashed up the place, stories say.

In the fields on the way back to Lough Ennell we disturbed a partridge shivering in ecstasy as she gave herself a dust bath, scooping floury drifts of powdered mud over her back with stubby wings. We were still looking for that special picnic spot, and found it at last on the footbridge over the Keoltown stream. Here we lay, cheese and brown bread in hand, staring down through gin-clear water at tendrils of lazily waving water weed, brilliantly green, trailing long strings of oxygen bubbles. If there's a dreamier spectacle to soothe a weary walker, I can't think what it might be.

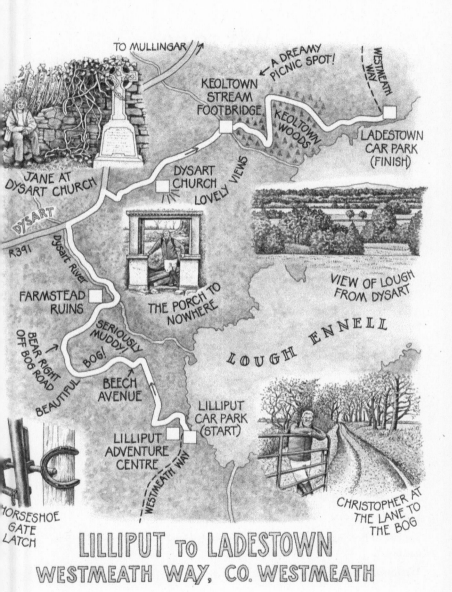

TO MULLINGAR

A DREAMY PICNIC SPOT!

WESTMEATH WAY

KEOLTOWN STREAM FOOTBRIDGE

KEOLTOWN WOODS

LADESTOWN CAR PARK (FINISH)

JANE AT DYSART CHURCH

DYSART CHURCH

LOVELY VIEWS

DYSART

R391

Dysart River

VIEW OF LOUGH FROM DYSART

THE PORCH TO NOWHERE

FARMSTEAD RUINS

L O U G H   E N N E L L

BEAR RIGHT OFF BOG ROAD

SERIOUSLY MUDDY BOG!

BEAUTIFUL

BEECH AVENUE

LILLIPUT CAR PARK (START)

LILLIPUT ADVENTURE CENTRE

WESTMEATH WAY

HORSESHOE GATE LATCH

CHRISTOPHER AT THE LANE TO THE BOG

LILLIPUT to LADESTOWN
WESTMEATH WAY, CO. WESTMEATH

169

WAY TO GO

MAP: OS of Ireland 1:50,000 Discovery 48; downloadable map/instructions (highly recommended) at www.discoverireland.ie/walking.

TRAVEL:

Rail (www.irishrail.ie) or bus (www.buseireann.ie) to Mullingar; then Mullingar Taxis (1800-600-800) or Ace Taxis (044-934-3333).

Road (two cars): Follow brown 'Lough Ennell/Ladestown' signs from R391 Mullingar-Clara; leave one car at Ladestown car park. Return in second car to R391; left towards Clara; follow brown 'Lilliput' signs to Lilliput car park.

WALK DIRECTIONS: At lake shore, left along track (yellow man/YM waymark) for ½ mile, through gate to road. Right for ½ mile; left (YM and Westmeath Way/WW fingerpost) along green lane which becomes gravel bog road. After almost a mile bear right on bend, off road through gate; very muddy track. At ruined settlement right across field; cross Dysart River; left along far bank (stiles, YM) to road. Right (WW – take care!); in ½ mile, right ('Lilliput'); on first right bend, left across bridge (WW). Follow lane past Dysart Church, on past farm buildings. Follow YM along right edge of garden; then down across fields (very boggy!) with hedge on right. Aim for left corner of wood ahead. Cross stream (YM); right to wood; left along its edge in 100 yards, right (YM), following YMs through Keoltown Woods, then along farm track, then lakeside drive to Ladestown car park.

LENGTH: 7 miles: allow 3–4 hours.

GRADE: Easy

CONDITIONS: Fields can be wet, muddy; boots/gaiters recommended.

DON'T MISS:
- views over Lough Ennell
- poignant farmstead ruins near Dysart River
- peaceful graveyard of Dysart Church

REFRESHMENTS: Picnic by Dysart River.

INFORMATION:

Tourist Office: Market Square, Mullingar (044-934-8650); www.discoverireland.ie eastcoast.

Westmeath Way booklet (enquire at TIC).

GIRLEY BOG,
CO MEATH

'WELL, I'LL BE DELIGHTED to walk over Girley Bog with you,' was Oliver Usher's decision. 'I've loved that bog all my life, and I just don't seem to tire of being there.'

That might have been a wee bit of an understatement. Observing the Kells antique dealer as he walked the squelching tracks of Girley Bog, not only naming this flower and that, yonder bird and the one beyond that, but taking the time to admire them and puzzle over their ways and means of thriving in the 'wet desert' of the County Meath bogland, Jane and I were privileged to see a true enthusiast at the fountainhead of his inspiration.

Oliver was a devotee of the bog, its secret treasures of wildlife and a beauty that only gradually reveals itself, back when such a sensibility was completely unfashionable. 'The bog? That's for cutting and burning, isn't it, or bringing the potatoes on?' You have to take a lot of time – a lifetime, really – to savour the bog as it should be savoured. Oliver has taken that time, and his reward has been endless interest, endless satisfaction, and a very keen desire to see his local Girley Bog, at all events, preserved from developers, road-builders, fly-tippers and all the other 'sure-it's-just-a-bit-of-waste-ground' merchants.

'The name's not really all that clever,' Oliver said as we started off along the rain-puddled track on a windy summer afternoon.

'Girley, *greathalloch* – a marshy place. I could have thought that one up!' The bog was certainly living up to its name today, but with boots and gaiters we kept the worst of the black splatter down at ankle level. Every ditch and drain glinted with water, and there was a constant background tinkle and trickle and occasional gurgle as if the bog itself were drinking.

There are several discrete sections to Girley Bog. The Coillte forestry lay in every stage of development from new plantings of tiny bright green spruce and pine saplings, through half-grown plantations to the tall dark 'corduroy battalions' of mature forest, and then to the tumbled ground and raw sawn stumps of recently harvested blocks. In the shadows under dwarf oak boughs we walked in a crepuscular half-light. Stands of scrub woodland planted by Mother Nature, silver birch and sallow, rang with birdsong: scratchy songs of long-tailed tits, *zip-zap!* of chiffchaffs, the liquid 'cut-price nightingale' of a blackcap, the expressive baritone of a missel thrush. Then there was the 'cutover' or old bog, square-cut for domestic fuel, now long abandoned and feathery with multiple grasses and wide white bursts of bog cotton.

'Now for the high bog!' announced Oliver, leading us off the track and into a fastness of uncut virgin bog. Girley Bog is a raised bog of thick heather and sphagnum moss, an increasingly rare environment in Ireland, feeding on rainwater rather than groundwater and slowly developing over thousands of years – perhaps ever since the end of the last Ice Age some 10,000 years ago. Out on this gently domed mass of bog, rising five or ten feet higher than the cutover, I had the sensation of being at sea, afloat on the back of a great grey wave under ecstatic lark song. We got down on our bellies and lost ourselves in a world of emerald green froglets, spotted orchids, minuscule lichens with scarlet heads like matchsticks, golden rods of bog asphodel and sundews engulfing motionless flies.

Among all these subtle, unemphatic delights, the one dramatic moment of the walk saved itself until last. As we were driving off, heading down the bog track to the Kells road, we noticed a tremendous commotion up ahead, an explosion of frantic energy and movement on the ground. Oliver cut the van's engine and we coasted up to the spot.

It was a magnificent male merlin, small and slate-backed, at death grips with a female blackbird almost his size. They rolled across the track almost under our wheels and fell into a bog drain, utterly intent on each other, the blackbird squawking desperately, the merlin clenching her breast in his talons and flapping his barred wings. Only when we got out of the van did the tiny hawk let go and fly off, leaving his victim exhausted and motionless in the ditch. It was a moment to remind us, if we needed reminding, of the natural world's never-ceasing redness in tooth and claw.

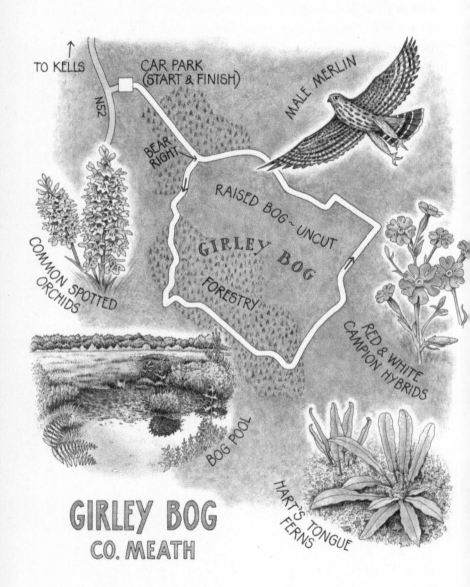

TO KELLS

N52

CAR PARK
(START & FINISH)

MALE MERLIN

BEAR
RIGHT

RAISED BOG ~ UNCUT

GIRLEY BOG

COMMON SPOTTED
ORCHIDS

FORESTRY

RED & WHITE
CAMPION HYBRIDS

BOG POOL

HART'S TONGUE
FERNS

GIRLEY BOG
CO. MEATH

WAY TO GO

MAP: OS of Ireland 1:50,000 Discovery 42; downloadable map/instructions (highly recommended) at www.discoverireland.ie/walking.

TRAVEL:

Bus (www.buseireann.ie): Services 108, 109 to Kells.

Road: From Kells, N52 towards Mullingar. After 4 miles, brown 'Trailhead' sign on left; gravelled track leads to car park (OSI ref N 695711).

WALK DIRECTIONS: Follow purple arrows (PA) along gravelled track to crossroads; right (PA) along bog path, following PA to make an anti-clockwise circuit of the bog.

LENGTH: 4 miles: allow 2 hours.

GRADE: Easy

CONDITIONS: Paths can be very squelchy, especially after rain; wear good waterproof boots.

DON'T MISS:

- subtle beauty of the uncut bog: birdsong, frogs, sundews, silence . . .
- tiny lichens, branched or scarlet-tipped – bring a magnifying glass
- wild food in season along the way: frochans, wild raspberries, blackberries

REFRESHMENTS: Picnic – and wild food!

INFORMATION:

Tourist Office: Castle Street, Trim; 046-943-7227; www.meath.ie/tourism.

35

BARNAVAVE, COOLEY PENINSULA, CO LOUTH

N O WONDER WILD QUEEN Medbh and her army from Connacht pitched camp in the hidden valley under Barnavave, high above Carlingford Lough. They must have been totally exhausted. They'd been up and down and round and about the Cooley Peninsula, searching for the elusive and ferocious Brown Bull, losing men to tempests, accidents and the strong right arm of Cúchulainn. So the *Táin Bó Cuailnge* tells us, at all events. That great epic is rather coy on the subject of the weather at the time, but no doubt rain fell and mist ribboned around the Cooley Mountains, then as now.

Rain and mist were certainly much in evidence today, hanging threateningly over Carlingford Lough and drawing a veil between the shores of the Republic and those of Northern Ireland. With Aude Laffon and her husband Peádar Quine as guides, philosophers and field archaeologists, Jane and I didn't really care. In the company of this young and enthusiastically knowledgeable couple, every dripping stone and foggy hilltop would have a tale to tell.

You could easily set off for a walk from Carlingford and never even leave the neatly white-washed town with its craggy old castles, its conversational shops and steamy-windowed pubs. It was a temptation to crowd the table in P.J. O'Hare's with pints, and let the hills go hang. But there was something fine about being the only souls out and about. The fuchsia bushes clinked silently with rain diamonds along the granite walls of the steep green lane above the town, and Slieve Foye hid its rugged face behind a gauze of mist as teasingly as any witchy queen of legend. Turning round for the view at the saddle of Golyin Pass, we watched the Mourne Mountains across Carlingford Lough change from milky green to a gauzy, moth-wing grey as the oncoming rain brushed them up in its skirts. A minute more and we had changed, too, from dry humans to glistening seals.

Looking west from the gap over the landscape of that earth-shaking struggle of arms and wills between Medbh and Cúchulainn, everything looked as insubstantial as a dream. Cloud curtains closed and opened between us and Windy Gap, gouged out in three days by Medbh's army as a gesture of contempt for Ulster. Rain seethed through the shallow valley of the River Cronn where famed Ualu drowned under his flagstone, and hundreds more Connachtmen with him. Even the peak of Barnavave, when we threaded the steep pass beneath it where queen and cohorts had camped, stood misted out of sight. Yet the old tale still held its magic.

Down in the throat of Medbh's Gap, as the rain began to fade off westward, we found an alignment of mossy stones in the crook of a wall. 'A court tomb,' Peádar said. 'But a very unusual one – it has two courts, one each end, see?' The two crab-claw shaped courts, perhaps built for funerary ceremonies, once guarded a great tomb with five internal chambers. It must have been a strong imperative that led hard-pressed subsistence hunters to build such a structure almost 7,000 years ago. How different were their lives, we wondered, from those pursued only a few decades ago in the abandoned village that lay a little way down the slope?

The stone-built houses stood roofless, huddled together along a tangle of cobbled lanes and bracken-smothered, ridged potato fields walled in against the salt wind and rain off Dundalk Bay. Fireplaces, stone-lined cupboards, a dog kennel delved into an outside wall – here were the intimate furnishings of a whole community, irrevocably wiped away. I followed the others down the lane towards Carlingford, picturing that vanished society, as far removed from our technological, hard-sell way of life as any brave old legend.

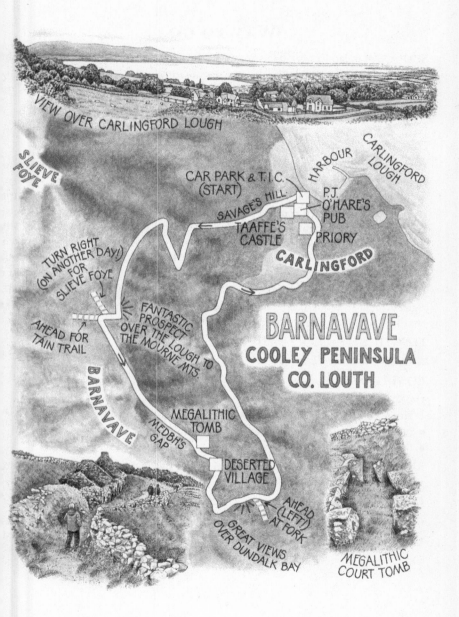

VIEW OVER CARLINGFORD LOUGH

SLIEVE FOYE

CARLINGFORD LOUGH

HARBOUR

CAR PARK & T.I.C. (START)

SAVAGE'S HILL

P.J. O'HARE'S PUB

TAAFFE'S CASTLE

PRIORY

CARLINGFORD

TURN RIGHT (ON ANOTHER DAY!) FOR SLIEVE FOYE

FANTASTIC PROSPECT OVER THE LOUGH TO THE MOURNE MTS.

AHEAD FOR TÁIN TRAIL

BARNAVAVE
COOLEY PENINSULA
CO. LOUTH

BARNAVAVE

MEDBH'S GAP

MEGALITHIC TOMB

DESERTED VILLAGE

AHEAD (LEFT) AT FORK

GREAT VIEWS OVER DUNDALK BAY

MEGALITHIC COURT TOMB

WAY TO GO

MAP: OS of Ireland 1:50,000 Discovery 36; downloadable map/instructions (highly recommended) soon to be available at www.discoverireland.ie/walking.

TRAVEL:

Bus: 161 Dundalk–Newry (www.buseireann.ie); 502, 701 (www.louthlinx.com).

Road: M1 to Dundalk; R173 to Carlingford. Main car park by Tourist Information Centre.

WALK DIRECTIONS: Walk past Taaffe's Castle to town square; up Savage's Hill (to right of Savage's Butchers). Where tarmac ends, head up walled green lane. Halfway up hill, track passes through gate on left and continues upward as green path. Turn right up Táin Way when you meet it (yellow 'walking man' marker). At pass, 'Slieve Foye' marker points right. In 50 m, Táin Way 'walking man' arrow points ahead; left here up fence towards Barnavave. Keep fence, then wall on right; steeply down Medbh's Gap. 50 m below left–right dogleg, right through wall (court tomb lies uphill in angle of wall). Path bears diagonally downhill to deserted village. Follow wall to right, then left by houses down walled lane. In 50 m, right between walls; in 100 m, right through wall; descend; left along lane. In ¼ mile, ahead (not right!) at fork; continue ¼ mile to tarmac road; left to Carlingford.

LENGTH: 5 miles: allow 3 hours.

GRADE: Moderate/Hard

CONDITIONS: Hill paths and tracks.

DON'T MISS:
- views from saddle over Carlingford Lough to Mourne Mountains
- megalithic tomb in Medbh's Gap
- deserted village

REFRESHMENTS: P.J. O'Hare's, Tholsel Street, Carlingford (042-937-3106; www pjoharescarlingford.com).

INFORMATION:

Carlingford Tourist Office: 042-937-3033; www.carlingford.ie.

Guided walks: Contact Aude Laffon; 0871-335159; www.setantatours.com.

36

CASTLE LAKE, BAILIEBOROUGH, CO CAVAN

'L ISTEN,' SAID JOHN ED Sheanon, indicating the shopfront of T.M. Smith Mortgages, 'there was a lady of that house who eloped with a Black and Tan – she never could come home again after that.' If you're after yarns about Bailieborough, take a walk with local butcher, tale teller and man of charm John Ed. Everyone knows John Ed around this neat, proud little plantation town in the heartland of County Cavan. 'Don't believe a word he tells you!' winked former schoolteacher Frank, passing by at the gates of St Anne's Church.

Jane and I were off with Jo Ed to walk around Bailieborough's Town and Castle Lakes. Peadar Reynolds, Bailieborough's keen local historian, had come along on this damp and blowy afternoon to add his fourpenn'orth, too. With its dress shops

and fruiterers, steamy cafés and old-fashioned hardware emporia, Bailieborough seems like a town that the Nasty Stick forgot to smack. On the outskirts of town we threaded the shore of the Town Lake, steely cold and wind-
ruffled, where a great crested grebe lay stock still on her nest among the rushes and allowed us a leisurely peep into her private world.

Cavan is a county well blessed with lakes. In fact they say that if you picked up Cavan and slapped it upside down on top of neighbouring Monaghan, the drumlin hills of the latter would fit exactly into the lakes of the former. Bailieborough boasts two lakes, the kidney-shaped Town Lake, and the straggling, thin-waisted Castle Lake a mile to the north. There was never a castle as such; the semi-fortified house built in the 1620s by Scottish planter William Bailie was known to locals as 'the Castle', and it lasted 300 years in various states of alteration on its eminence outside the town that William built.

We followed a boreen lined with tall foxgloves, under fine beech trees and on into the former castle demesne, immaculately maintained these days by forester Bernard McManus. Fed by snaking rivers and streams, Castle Lake gleamed between the trees. 'I was walking here last year,' said Peadar, 'and heard a great splashing, and it was two otters playing in the stream. What fun they were having!'

Round at the head of the lake a pair of swans was busy shepherding their brood of seven cygnets.

We went on along the shore to where a side track led away among the trees. Up there the Hanging Tree stood stark under a weight of ivy. 'Lord Lisgar's men hanged a boy from that tree for cutting timber,' John Ed told us, 'and the mother cursed Lisgar so that he would have no heirs to follow him in Castle House. And he never did.'

Beyond the Hanging Tree lay the ruins of Castle House, a fragment of stone walls tumbled under mats of honeysuckle. The house played host to a group of Marist Brothers during the early 20th century, but once they had gone from the place it quickly deteriorated. In a tangle of laurels not far away we found their stone-walled cemetery. Seven graves in a row among the bushes; seven ornate crosses; seven modest inscriptions recording the passing of Brothers Owen, Benedict, Justin, Swithen, Dermott and William, alongside Brother Andrew, known as 'Stability', 58 years a member of the community. As we left the graves a big wind got up and sighed in the treetops – a very apt and poignant moment in the quiet woodland.

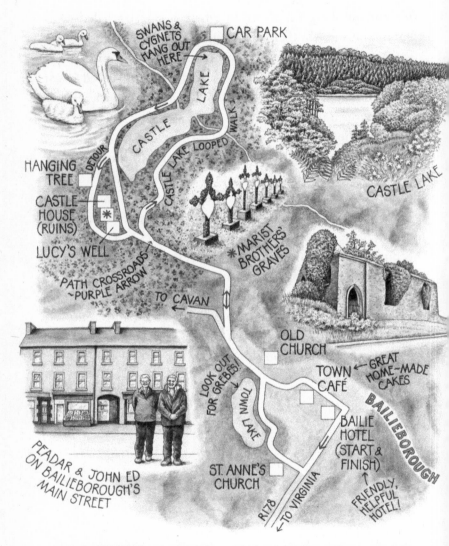

SWANS & CYGNETS HANG OUT HERE

CAR PARK

CASTLE LAKE

CASTLE LAKE LOOPED WALK

DETOUR

HANGING TREE

CASTLE HOUSE (RUINS)

LUCY'S WELL

PATH CROSSROADS ~PURPLE ARROW

MARIST BROTHERS' GRAVES

CASTLE LAKE

TO CAVAN

OLD CHURCH

TOWN CAFÉ ← GREAT HOME-MADE CAKES

BAILIE HOTEL (START & FINISH)

BAILIEBOROUGH

FRIENDLY, HELPFUL HOTEL!

LOOK OUT FOR GREBES!

TOWN LAKE

PEADAR & JOHN ED ON BAILIEBOROUGH'S MAIN STREET

ST. ANNE'S CHURCH

R178 ← TO VIRGINIA

CASTLE LAKE, BAILIEBOROUGH
CO. CAVAN

WAY TO GO

MAP: OS of Ireland 1:50,000 Discovery 35; downloadable map/instructions (highly recommended) at www.discoverireland.ie/walking.

TRAVEL:

Bus (www.buseireann.ie): services 108, 166 to Bailieborough.

Road: Bailieborough is signed off N3 Navan–Cavan road at Virginia. Park in Main Street.

WALK DIRECTIONS: Follow R178 Virginia road past library. In 500 m, right through gates, past St Anne's Church. Cross Chapel Road; follow path by Town Lake. Left along Cavan Road for 500 m. At 50 kmh sign before left bend, follow pavement to right. In 30 m, left by bungalow, past metal barrier. Follow track into castle demesne. In ⅔ mile, reach path crossroads. Turn right (direction arrow). From here, Official Looped Walk circles Castle Lake.

Castle House ruin and Marist Brothers' graves detour: follow Looped Walk round Castle Lake for 1¾ miles (passing car park). At 'Castle' signpost on left, right up gravel track for 500 m to crossing of tracks at Hanging Tree. Right for 200 m to metal barrier on right; left for 200 m to Castle House ruins. Retrace steps; left by barrier, downhill for 200 m to T-junction of tracks. Left for 400 m to return to Looped Walk track, detouring left up bank to see Marist Brothers' cemetery.

Rejoin Looped Walk (blue arrow); right to cross river and reach path crossroads at direction arrow; forward to retrace steps to Bailieborough.

LENGTH: 5 miles: allow 2–3 hours.

GRADE: Easy

DON'T MISS:
- swans and cygnets at Castle Lake car park
- Marist Brothers' cemetery

REFRESHMENTS: Town Café, Main Street, Bailieborough (042-967-5589) – home-made cake and tarts.

INFORMATION:

Cavan Tourist Office, Fernham Street, Cavan; 049-433-1942; www.cavantourism.com.

Bailieborough, A Plantation Market Town – town trail booklet, widely available locally (Bailieborough Development Association, 042-969-4716; www.bailieborough.com).

Local Walks around Bailieborough: Wednesday evenings – contact John Ed Sheanon on 042-966-5342.

37

ROSSMORE LAKES, CO MONAGHAN

MIST SIFTED THROUGH THE Monaghan lanes and hung thick among the redwoods, pines and spruce trees of Rossmore Forest Park. A pair of swans sailed like two white boats on Castle Lake, effortlessly graceful in that unconscious way swans have. Jane and I threaded the tanglewood of a rhododendron tunnel towards a glow of pearly light, catching those magical glimpses so typical of a misty winter's afternoon – swan down circling in an eddy, a mossy bough in a birch swamp, leafless twigs suspended weightless and without substantial form in the vaporous air.

It's been half a century since the Earls of Rossmore quit their castle and lake-indented lands on the outskirts of Monaghan town. The Coillte-owned woods stand full of grand trees. At the foot of Priestfield Lake, where lianas and half-drowned pines made serpent loops in the water, we came upon the shaggy spire of a giant redwood disappearing overhead into the mist. A modest obelisk recorded the planting of the tree by Henry Cairnes Westenra, 4th Lord Rossmore, on his 11th birthday in 1862. Henry died young, and was succeeded by his brother Derrick, 5th Lord Rossmore, a 'hot-headed, rather foolish youth, a noted patron of the turf'. Derrick was a chum of Edward, Prince of Wales, at a time when that jolly gentleman was being kept waiting for his accession to the throne by his mother Victoria's inconvenient propensity to continue living. Wherever the Prince went to stay, shooting parties, port, cigars and assignations were sure to follow, and Derrick certainly enjoyed his full share.

We passed the fern-sprouting ruin of Lady Rossmore's Cottage, its interior sunk in moss and drifts of sycamore leaves, and went on through the foggy woods, kicking up leaf showers to release a rank stink of fox. Deep among the trees near Barnhill Lake lay a tumble of mossy stones – a court tomb, perhaps 5,000 years old, silent and seldom visited. The walk led on between the Twin Lakes, their banks and waters all but invisible in the late afternoon's thickening mist. A moody, melancholic stroll.

Up on the empty terraces of Rossmore Castle in the murky twilight we found five flights of steps and a castellated turret. They are all that remains of one of Ireland's most extravagant Big Houses, built in 1827 by Henry Westenra, 3rd Lord Rossmore, in tremendous Gothic style. Not everyone was thrilled with the plans. 'The idea of transforming the beautiful face of our gracefully sloping hill,' Rossmore's own son was

moved to comment, 'with grotesque terraces, straight lines and mathematical walks – the point of the compasses ought to be poked into the eye of the fellow that proposed it.' However, the castle went ahead and, like Topsy, it growed, becoming a fabulous confection of towers and turrets, pepperpots and candle-snuffers, oriel windows and crow-stepped battlements.

If you're going to build a castle, you might as well go for it big style. In 1858 Rossmore Castle was further extended. The number and variety of its windows caused much comment – at the final count there were 117 windows, in 53 separate styles. The drawing room, enlarged no fewer than five times, was so capacious it bulged the whole building out at one side. This mega-room was the result of a contest between the Rossmores and their neighbours and rivals the Shirleys of Lough Fea, to see who could boast possession of the largest room in County Monaghan. Notwithstanding Rossmore's monstrous drawing room, it was Shirley who scooped the bays with a Great Hall completed by a minstrels' gallery and a giant beamed roof.

After its glorious heyday, the castle fell to the mundane affliction of dry rot, and was demolished in 1972. The Rossmores' run-down estate was parcelled out between local farmers and the Forestry. Jane and I paced the terraces and the steps in the misty half dark of evening, and I swear I could hear, out on the brink of belief, the swish of silk dresses and the rumble of cigar-smoke laughter.

TO CLONES N54

MONAGHAN

R189

RHODODENDRON TUNNEL

TWIN LAKES

FOREST PARK ENTRANCE

BARNHILL LAKE

COURT TOMB

WOODLAND STREAM

TO NEWBLISS

R189

CAR PARK (START)

CASTLE LAKE

SITE OF ROSSMORE CASTLE

PRIESTFIELD LAKE

LADY ROSSMORE'S COTTAGE (RUIN)

ARDAGHY LOUGH

* THE 4TH EARL'S GIANT REDWOOD (1862)

BARTLE'S LOUGH

STEENSON'S LOUGH

ROSSMORE LAKES
CO. MONAGHAN

ROSSMORE CASTLE STEPS

WAY TO GO

MAP: OS of Ireland 1:50,000 Discovery 28; downloadable map/instructions at www.discoverireland.ie/walking and www.coillteoutdoors.ie.

TRAVEL:

From Monaghan town, N54 Clones road; in 1 mile, left on R189 ('Newbliss'). In ¾ mile, Rossmore Forest Park entrance on left; follow road to car park.

WALK DIRECTIONS: From car park, follow brown 'Lakes Walk' sign across footbridge. Right, then left (white arrows/WA) up path beside toilets. Bear right around Castle Lake to T-junction. Left (WA) for 300 m to pass pointed wooden post. Keep forward for 100 m to cross track and reach Castle site. Return to pointed post; bear left and follow WA around Lakes Loop. Approaching Barnhill Lake, bear right (WA) at a 'Cootehill Road' sign; follow path for 200 m; left (black post) for 50 m; left (brown 'Court Tomb' fingerpost) on boggy track through trees for 150 m to find court tomb. Return to 'Cootehill Road' sign; resume Lakes Walk to its end at car park.

LENGTH: 5 miles/8 km: allow 2–2½ hours.

GRADE: Easy

DON'T MISS:
- Castle site
- superb views over the lakes
- court tomb

REFRESHMENTS: None en route – take a picnic.

INFORMATION:

Monaghan Tourist Office: Mullacroghery, Clones Road; 047-81122; www. discoverireland.ie/northwest.

38

SLIABH AN IARAINN, AGHACASHEL, CO LEITRIM

I T ISN'T EVERY WALK that we start with a drive in a Rolls-Royce Silver Shadow. Actually, for 'we', read 'Jane'. She was the lucky divil lounging back on the blue leather seats. When you order a taxi, you don't expect a Roller to pitch up. But that's the sort of magic that can happen up in County Leitrim – especially if you're in the company of local guru, historian, piper and man of knowledge Jackie Lee.

As chance would have it, Jackie's chum John Burke found he had an hour to fill before wafting a lucky Sligo bride to her wedding in his beautiful car. So it was in the Silver Shadow that John drove Jane and Jackie from Drumshanbo up towards Sliabh an Iarainn, the Iron Mountain, our target for today. And I was the baggage donkey, eating their dust in my shuddering old jalopy. Ah, well . . .

In his post office shop at Aghacashel in the shadow of Sliabh an Iarainn, Jackie dispenses walks leaflets, sound advice and picnic goodies to all comers. We collected some of each, and he waved us off up the mountain road.

It's a long time since they mined the iron on Sliabh an Iarainn that went to make Ha'penny Bridge in Dublin. A few of the old scars remain in the long line of cliffs that stand bared like green-grey teeth towards the east. The miners and herding families of the mountain eked a tough living, and the Famine struck hard hereabouts. On a bleak hillside at Mullaghgarve the local victims lie buried, a polished marble slab their memorial; and higher up the mountain a commemorative seat stands by the track.

From here the Iron Mountain looked formidable, a fortress-like escarpment topped with an olive-coloured dome of bog still streaked and patched with spring snow. But once we had gained more height and turned off through squelching bog to follow the feet of the cliffs, we saw how the wall of rock was in fact broken into pinnacles and gullies. The Mass Rock of Sliabh an Iarainn is so cleverly concealed behind its tall pinnacle that we'd have missed it altogether if Jackie Lee hadn't told us where to look for the rough-cut steps. The shadow of furtive Masses lies thick in the cleft, the celebrant trying to keep his mind on the mysteries, his flock glancing fearfully through the crack in the rock for spies or soldiers.

A ghost-white hen harrier came gliding along the cliffs on

stiff black-tipped wings. We scrambled up through the outcrop and turned along the edge of the cliffs. Picnic time, sitting on rocks flaky with orange and black ironstone. An immense view opened south and east over lakes, smoky blue lowlands and hummocks of peaks.

A mountain spring, black and ice-cold, came sliding beneath a white snow bridge to tumble down its cleft. We traced its course up over the snow banks, and then struck out across a great dome of bare brown moorland. Somewhere in this sodden

and half-eroded wilderness was the Ordnance Survey point that marked the summit of Sliabh an Iarainn. We stumbled across it by chance, a concrete slab with an iron plate set in it, distinguishing one turf tussock from all the rest. A vast sunlit view – every lake, field, wood and mountain for 100 miles from Donegal to Sligo, Leitrim to the Midlands. It was a celestial prospect, and we stood at the crown of the Iron Mountain and stared as if we'd never leave the place.

SLIABH AN IARAINN
AGHACASHEL, CO. LEITRIM

LOUGH ALLEN

VIEW FROM MASS ROCK

JANE ON THE SUMMIT MARKER

SLIABH AN IARAINN

SUMMIT MARKER (585m)

SUPERB PANORAMA ALL ROUND!

CHUNK OF IRON ON THE IRON MOUNTAIN

GREAT PICNIC SPOT!

STEEP DESCENT ON RETURN~ SLIDE ON YOUR BOTTOM

BEAR LEFT ACROSS STREAM

TURN LEFT UPHILL BY STREAM

MASS ROCK

HIDDEN BEHIND PINNACLE!

MULLAGH-GARVE FAMINE GRAVEYARD

SCRAMBLE UP THE ROCKS!

FAMINE MEMORIAL SEAT

MASS ROCK

TO DRUMSHANBO

AGHACASH POST OFFIC SHOP (START)

CHRISTOPHER AT THE FAMINE SEAT

WAY TO GO

MAP: OS of Ireland 1:50,000 Discovery 26; downloadable map/instructions (highly recommended) at www.discoverireland.ie/walking.

TRAVEL:

Bus (www.buseireann.ie): 469 Sligo–Longford or 462 Carrigallen–Sligo to Drumshanbo; then taxi (071-964-1040 or 1585 – 4½ miles)

Road: R207, R208 to Drumshanbo; minor road from village centre to Aghacashel PO (OS of I ref 045135). Please ask permission to park!

WALK DIRECTIONS: From PO, back up road for 100 yards; right up mountain road for 1¼ miles; through gate by Famine memorial seat (032147). Uphill ('G' waymarkers) for ½ mile through 2 more gates; then left across footbridge (025153). Follow 'G's (boggy ground!) to base of cliffs. Pass pinnacle; look back to see steps up to Mass Rock. 'G's run out here; continue along base of escarpment to end; turn right up through rocks (a bit of scrambling) to top. Right along cliff edge (take care!) for ½ mile to cross fence and stream in gully. Left uphill along fence, then bear right to summit (019159 – concrete square with iron plaque on 'island' in 'sea' of peat!) Return to fence; left downhill; recross fence; very steeply down with fence on left (take care!) to track; return to Aghacashel. Detour to Mullaghgarve Famine graveyard: ½ mile below Famine memorial seat, left (037140) for ⅓ mile; cross stream; left to graveyard and memorial (040145).

LENGTH: 5½ miles: allow 3–4 hours.

GRADE: Hard

CONDITIONS: Boggy in parts; a little scrambling; cliff edges; one short, steep descent. Hill-walking gear, boots. Avoid in mist, heavy rain.

DON'T MISS:
- Mass Rock behind pinnacle
- views from the summit
- Mullaghgarve Famine graveyard

REFRESHMENTS: None en route – take a picnic.

INFORMATION:

Carrick-on-Shannon Tourist Office: 071-962-0170; www.enjoyleitrim.ie.

Jackie Lee: Aghacashel PO (071-964-1569).

Guide books/leaflets: Pack of local walks, available from Aghacashel PO; www.leitrimwalks.com.

39
THE ROSSES, CO SLIGO

'ROSSES IS A LITTLE sea-dividing, sandy plain, covered with short grass, like a green table-cloth, and lying in the foam midway between the round cairn-headed Knocknarea and 'Ben Bulben, famous for hawks':

> But for Ben Bulben and Knocknarea,
> Many a poor sailor'd be cast away,

as the rhyme goes.'

That was the Rosses of Sligo as William Butler Yeats described them in *The Celtic Twilight*. W.B. knew a thing or two about rhymes, and he and his kid brother Jack certainly knew the Rosses, the sandy peninsula between Sligo Harbour and Drumcliff Bay, like the backs of their hands. Their mother Susan Pollexfen was a Sligo woman, and the Dublin-reared lads would often come to spend weeks at a time with their grandparents when money got tight. The wild shores around Sligo Bay, and the table-topped mountains of Benbulben and Knocknarea that were always in sight as landmarks from the coast, proved a life-long inspiration to the brothers.

Later in life, poet William and painter Jack would each acknowledge the 'thought of Sligo' that pervaded all their work. It was William who told the world about the Sligo legends of Knocknarea where rapacious Queen Medbh lies buried, and of Benbulben on whose slopes mighty Fionn MacCumhaill took a deadly revenge on his cuckolder Diarmuid. Jack, meanwhile, put ghosts and mysteries into the lonely strands and drifting figures of the Rosses with his loose, expressionist paintbrush.

On a windy morning of freckling drizzle, with more rain forecast from the sea, Jane and I struggled into wet weather gear on the seafront at Rosses Point. Niall Bruton's haunting sculpture 'Waiting on Shore' stood facing the open Atlantic – a woman in wind-whipped skirts, her arms stretching seaward, archetype of the wives of Rosses fishermen down the ages. Her counterpoint the Metal Man, rigged out in 19th-century naval officer's uniform, straddled offshore in the narrows opposite Deadman's Point, his outflung arm pointing ships to the safe channel up to Sligo's quays. Beyond man and woman rose the humpback of Knocknarea, the wild queen's cairn standing proud on top under smoking cloud. Inland, though, Benbulben and its fellow mountains were hidden from the feet up.

Down on the long west-facing strand a few brave souls in billowing anoraks were battling the wind and spray. We strode out fast along the rain-pocked sands, boots crackling over dried ribbon weed, mussel shells and crab claws hollowed out by gulls, whose melancholy, whinging cries gave a bitter-sweet edge to the morning. Kidney vetch, harebells and tiny bushes of wild roses studded the dunes and low crumbly cliffs. Halfway along the beach, two surf-buggyists stood in contemplation of a giant dome of rusty cast iron, half-buried in the sand. 'A boiler?' one mused. 'Or a buoy, d'you think?' The other shook his long locks decisively. 'Nope. A spaceship.'

Across the neck of the golf course we went, and down on to the long dune spit of the Low Rosses. Stars of insectivorous butterwort made lime-green rosettes in patches of sphagnum bog. The delicate silvery chrysalises of six-spot burnet moths were anchored to the stalks of marram grass, and the moths themselves in tar-black and crimson clung to the flowerheads of harebells and pyramidal orchids while they waited for the rain to die off. That wasn't going to happen any time soon.

'At the northern corner of Rosses,' wrote William Yeats in *The Celtic Twilight*, 'is a little promontory of rocks and sand and grass: a mournful, haunted place. Few countrymen would fall asleep under its low cliff, for he who sleeps here may wake "silly", the Sidhe having carried off his soul. There is no more ready short-cut to the dim kingdom than this plovery headland.'

Out at the far point we lingered, looking across Drumcliff Bay towards Lissadell, delighting in the rainy solitude of time and place. Most poignant and beautiful of all of Jack Yeats's mystical late paintings, *Leaving the Far Point* has its setting out here. It must have been just this sort of weather – misty, windy and seething with sea rain – that Yeats had in mind when he shadowed out those figures of himself, his wife Cottie and Uncle George Pollexfen, as transparent as ghosts, walking the wet sands of Rosses Point on another wild day long ago.

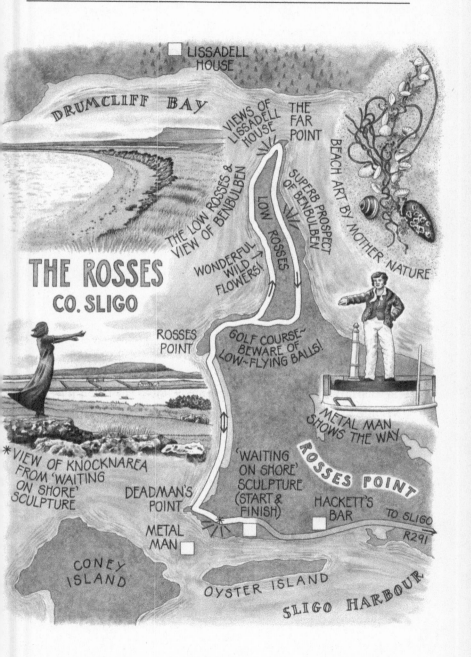

LISSADELL HOUSE

DRUMCLIFF BAY

VIEWS OF LISSADELL HOUSE

THE FAR POINT

BEACH ART BY MOTHER NATURE

THE LOW ROSSES & VIEW OF BENBULBEN

SUPERB PROSPECT OF BENBULBEN

LOW ROSSES

THE ROSSES
CO. SLIGO

WONDERFUL WILD FLOWERS!

ROSSES POINT

GOLF COURSE~ BEWARE OF LOW~FLYING BALLS!

METAL MAN SHOWS THE WAY

ROSSES POINT

*VIEW OF KNOCKNAREA FROM 'WAITING ON SHORE' SCULPTURE

DEADMAN'S POINT

'WAITING ON SHORE' SCULPTURE (START & FINISH)

HACKETT'S BAR

TO SLIGO

R291

METAL MAN

CONEY ISLAND

OYSTER ISLAND

SLIGO HARBOUR

199

WAY TO GO

MAP: OS of Ireland 1:50,000 Discovery 16.

TRAVEL:

Rail (www.irishrail.ie) to Sligo.

Bus (www.buseireann.ie): Service 473 from Sligo.

Road: N15 or N16 to Sligo; R291 to Rosses Point. By 'Waiting On Shore' statue, left to car park above lifeboat station.

WALK DIRECTIONS: Follow tarred path towards sea; then follow cliff path and strand to Rosses Point. Cross side of golf course (watch out for flying balls!), keeping to cliff edge path. Continue clockwise around Low Rosses sandspit. Return across neck of spit to Rosses Point; retrace steps to car park.

LENGTH: 6 miles: allow 2–3 hours.

GRADE: Easy

CONDITIONS: Cliff paths, sandy beach.

DON'T MISS:
- Metal Man and his Consort
- views of Knocknarea and Benbulben
- flowers of the Low Rosses

REFRESHMENTS: Hackett's Bar on seafront, Rosses Point (071-917-7142).

INFORMATION:

Tourist Office: Temple Street, Sligo; 071-914-1905; www.discoverireland.ie/northwest.

Jack Yeats Collection: Model Arts and Niland Gallery (www.modelart.ie), Sligo. Paintings online: http://www.artcyclopedia.com/artists/yeats_jack_b.html.

Walking tour operators, local walks including Discover Ireland's National Loop Walks, walking festivals throughout Ireland: www.discoverireland.ie/walking; www.coillteoutdoors.ie.

40

TOWER LOOP, GLENCOLUMBKILLE, CO DONEGAL

N O MATTER WHICH DIRECTION a traveller comes from, the final approach to Glencolumbkille is made across swathes of stark bogland. From this sombre setting, an archetypal west Donegal landscape of great but harsh beauty, the shock of the plunge into the long, sheltered green valley running due east inland between two high, rugged headlands had Jane and me gasping. We'd hardly pulled up at An Chistin café before Inga Bock, Donegal's Rural Recreation Officer, suited and booted for hill walking, was at the car door with a big enthusiastic grin.

Poor Jane! It was Hobson's choice for her – the exhilaration of high striding, of windy cliffs and giant views, versus the solitary bliss of an afternoon's fossicking on the wild beaches of Glen Bay. The pull of the sea, always there in her heart and soul, proved the stronger. Off she went to the shore where Atlantic rollers were crashing, while Inga and I faced for the hillside, climbing up above the farm of Bíofán to the enormous cairn at the saddle that marks the rough stone-built well of St Columbkille. Offerings and leavings had been squeezed into every interstice above the still, clear water in the basin: crucifixes, rosary beads, keys, rings, delicately articulated mouse bones. Here we sat, looking back over the village in its green glen and listening to the sigh of waves on the sands of Skelpoonagh Bay below.

Glencolumbkille lies studded with monoliths, stone circles, ancient tombs and sacred wells. The remote western glen must have been a powerful magnet for worship and spirituality thousands of years before Columb, the Donegal boy with the holy burden on him, came here to establish a monastery in the middle of the 6th century AD. The saint and his acolytes blessed the wells and the stones.

Columb was soon gone, following his destiny across the sea to Iona and the establishment of a Celtic church that would last a thousand years. He left behind him in Glencolumbkille an imperishable aura. His followers incised the standing stones with mazy crucifixes. They erected crosses and built tiny cell-like churches, still scattered across the valley cheek by jowl with the monuments of prehistoric belief. In Glencolumbkille, as much as anywhere in Ireland, one senses the intermingling of an old and a far older faith.

And what was a nice girl from the Frisian Islands doing in a place like this? 'Oh,' said Inga as we climbed on up the mountain track, 'I came to Ireland 20 years ago to help start a riding school. "I'll just stop here and look around a little before I go back to Germany," is what I told myself. Well – the going back never happened!'

The old track rose across a wide upland of black turf and purple-bronze heather. A blasting south-west wind shoved us on, up to the gaunt old signal tower built on Glen Head early in the 19th century. Napoleon never came, but the tower still stands, outfacing the storms.

Here we looked out across a sea whipped by the wind into long white lanes of foam. It was too blusterous to stay there long. With the impatient hand of the gale as a propeller we sped on along the sparkling mica rocks of the track, over the crest of Beefan and Garveross Mountain, past turf banks undercut by wind and rain into the semblance of ragged neolithic tombs. The view on the descent was a mighty one, all the way across the glen where the Slieve League cliffs rose in a great green wave to their 2,000-foot plunge into the sea.

Jane beat us into An Chistin by a short head, having roamed the beaches to her heart's content. We looked at each other and laughed. Her cheeks were pink, her hair was a salty tangle. Inga had wind tears in her eyes. My beard was full of turf fragments. What a wind; what a great day.

TOWER LOOP, GLENCOLUMBKILLE
CO. DONEGAL

GLEN HEAD

SIGNAL
TOWER

BEEFAN & GARVEROSS
MOUNTAIN

CROSS PILLAR

ST.
COLUMBKILLE'S
WELL

AN CLOCHÁN

SKELPOONAGH BAY

BÍOFÁN
FARM

CROSS
PILLAR

*IONAD
SIÚL
CENTRE
(START &
FINISH)

GLEN BAY

AN CHISTIN
CAFÉ

CHURCH

R263

GLENCOLUMBKILLE

Murlin River

VIEW OVER GLEN BAY &
SKELPOONAGH BAY WITH INGA

TO KILLYBEGS

WAY TO GO

MAP: OS of Ireland 1:50,000 Discovery 10; downloadable map/instructions (highly recommended) at www.discoverireland.ie/walking.

TRAVEL:

Bus (www.buseireann.ie): Service 490 from Donegal Town; or McGeehan Coaches (074-954-6150; www.mgbus.com).

Road: N56 Donegal Town–Killybegs; R263 to Glencolumbkille.

WALK DIRECTIONS: Starting from Ionad Siúl Hill Walkers' Centre, fork left at memorial; follow blue arrows along road and up to Bíofán Farm (OSI ref G 525859). To visit St Columbkille's Well (525861), follow markers uphill to right; then join mountain track and climb to post with arrows (524866). Left to tower (519869); return to track; follow blue arrows for 1 mile uphill over Beefan & Garveross Mountain to road (536862). Right downhill for 1 mile to T-junction by St Columbkille's Church (536849). Left past church and cross pillar to Ionad Siúl.

LENGTH: 5 miles: allow 2½–3 hours.

GRADE: Moderate

CONDITIONS: Steeply up to signal tower; some boggy patches.

DON'T MISS:

- St Columbkille's Well
- valley and sea views from signal tower and mountain
- cross pillar near St Columbkille's Church

REFRESHMENTS: An Chistin café, Glencolumbkille (074-973-0213); ring for opening times.

INFORMATION:

Tourist Office: The Quay, Donegal; 074-972-1148; www.discoverireland.ie/north west.

Glencolumbkille Folk Village Museum: 074-973-0017; www.glenfolkvillage.com.

41

GLENVEAGH NATIONAL PARK, CO DONEGAL

THE HERALDIC DEER ON the gateposts gazed fixedly at one another as I passed between them. Maybe it was the early morning hour, but I could have sworn the left-hand stag was curling his lip, while his fellow guardian of the drive to Glenveagh Castle looked momentarily as though a bad smell had brushed his distended nostrils. With their heads held high, and a pair of real antlers fixed in each stone brow, they exuded aristocratic disdain. But that was nothing to the glare of utter disgust I received half a mile further on from the big red stag who had somehow got himself down to the shore of Lough Veagh below the drive. I'm sure he should have been safely on guard with his posse over on the wide moors of Derrylahan beyond the lough. Whatever about that, he gave a snort and cantered off, rolling his eye back to keep me under observation.

Glenveagh National Park is the pride and joy of County Donegal, a haven not only for Ireland's largest herd of red deer but for plants, trees, bog insects, birds and anyone of the human persuasion who loves these things. You'll rarely walk in a more carefully preserved landscape than this. Glenveagh was acquired by the Irish nation in the 1970s and 80s after more than a century of being managed as a private sporting estate, and its mountains and lakes retain an atmosphere of existing in some delightful time-warp outside the modern world.

I strolled by the dark waters of Lough Veagh, looking out across the lake to the lumpy spine of the Derryveagh Mountains, until the turrets of Glenveagh Castle peeped out of their trees ahead. The path led through sunken gardens and flowery dells to the massive granite walls of the castle – no medieval stronghold, but a fine Big House built in Scottish baronial style in 1870–3 by one of the harshest of all landlords, John Adair. Inside the grim keep, Adair had a luxurious country-house interior installed. He was notorious for having evicted 244 of his tenants in the bleak winter of 1861, in order to incorporate their land in his park. But when it came to pleasing his new American wife, Cornelia, no expense was spared.

Back along the beautiful loughside, I went down from the Visitor Centre through a Scots pine wood to emerge in the wild moorland of Derrylahan, cradled in sunlit mountains of such beauty it made me gasp. Pink fairy bonnets of lousewort spattered the bog. An electric blue dragonfly manifested itself in front of my nose, hovered there a second, then dematerialised, to reappear by magic a few feet away. Then the red deer appeared, two dozen of them, trotting with easy grace over the hillside beyond a stunted oakwood.

It was Cornelia Adair who established the red deer herd at Glenveagh after John Adair died in 1885. Local people liked her as much as they had despised her arrogant husband, it's said. After he was gone she enhanced the little kingdom of Glenveagh with flowers, trees and the free-running deer, and everyone is the beneficiary of that generous vision today.

WAY TO GO

MAP: OS of Ireland 1:50,000 Discovery 6; map/instructions in Visitors' Guide.

TRAVEL:

Glenveagh National Park Visitor Centre is signposted on the R251 Gweedore–Letterkenny road, 10 miles/16 km east of Dunlewy.

NB A shuttle bus service (€2) operates between Glenveagh Visitor Centre and Glenveagh castle.

WALK DIRECTIONS: From Glenveagh National Park Visitor Centre, turn left along tarmac drive. Pass to left of National Park headquarters, and follow drive between entrance gateposts, then beside Lough Veagh for 1½ miles to reach gates to Glenveagh Castle grounds. Go through, and follow paths through gardens to reach castle.

Return along drive to car park, and join the Derrylahan Trail (detailed in Glenveagh National Park Visitors' Guide), with numbered guide posts. Turn left between two boulders on to path that descends through trees. Go through gate and follow path through Scots pine wood, until it leaves wood through forest gate. 30 m beyond gate, turn left along path. In another 100 m it forks; don't take rough track that climbs straight ahead, but bear right along lower, grassy track into sedgy hollow. The gravelled path steepens to climb through a little wood and run east across moor to meet a fence. Bear right along fence; then, halfway to trees ahead, turn left through a deer gate in fence to reach a road. Right to return to car park.

LENGTH: 5 miles: allow 2½ hours.

GRADE: Easy

CONDITIONS: Boggy underfoot in some of the hollows and on the moor of Derrylahan; otherwise fine underfoot.

DON'T MISS:
- Glenveagh Castle and gardens
- the red deer of Derrylahan
- fantastic views along Lough Veagh

REFRESHMENTS: Tearoom at castle (open Easter and June–September); restaurant at the Visitor Centre.

Cont.

INFORMATION:

Tourist Office: Neil T. Blaney Road, Letterkenny; 074-912-1160; www.discover ireland.ie/donegal.

Visitors' Guide, Castle Gardens guide and more, available at Glenveagh Visitor Centre.

Glenveagh National Park: 074-913-7090, ext. 3608/9; www.glenveaghnationalpark.ie. open all year except Good Friday and Christmas week, 10–6 Mar–Oct, 10–5 Oct– Mar. Park and Visitor Centre: entrance free.

Glenveagh Castle: Castle gardens: entrance free. Castle Guided Tour: €3.

42

BURNS MOUNTAIN AND BANAGHER HILL CIRCUIT, BLUE STACK MOUNTAINS, CO DONEGAL

IS THERE A DREAMIER landscape, or name, than that of the Blue Stack Mountains? My God, Donegal people have scooped the lottery when it comes to walking country – a range of magnificently crumpled mountains reflected in the glassy, island-dotted waters of Lough Eske under a sky where golden eagles soar, a fine and friendly hotel at Harvey's Point to admire it all from, and a guide as knowledgeable as Pat Murphy to winkle out the crabmeat of walking delights from the shell of a perfect day. Some folk have all the luck.

I felt pretty lucky myself, setting out from Harvey's Point in company with Pat on a peerless blue morning – certainly luckier than the poor wretches who clustered round the Famine Pot in the 1840s. What a gulf lies between those days and these. The great iron cauldron with its thick spout stands in a display shelter by the roadside, not far from the spring where Quaker benefactors set it up to boil cornmeal stirabout for the feeding of five times five thousand starving people. A humbling image

211

for the well-fed walker with bacon and eggs in his belly.

A country lane skirts the feet of Burns Mountain, rising gradually to reveal a wonderful view south-west to the Sligo mountains and the sandspits round Rossknowlagh and Ballyshannon, all pale blue today with the blur of heat and distance. We climbed a stony lane hemmed with dandelions, coltsfoot and the last remnants of the spring's celandines. 'Country medicine used to be based on the idea that a plant would benefit the thing it looked like,' remarked Pat. 'Celandines have these knobby roots, see? They put the English in mind of a bunch of haemorrhoids, so they called the celandine 'pilewort' and used it to cure piles. But the Irish thought it looked like a cow's teats, so they'd hang it over the byre to bring on the milk.'

Mountain shapes pushed up along the skyline as we climbed – the round head of snow-streaked Binn an tSruthaill behind the petrified wave of Banagher, tent-shaped Carnaween across the deep Eglish valley. Locals still climb Carnaween on the first Sunday of June to say a prayer and cast a stone on to the summit cairn. In olden times, that was a sure-fire charm for meeting a sweetheart among folk ascending the peak from other valleys round about. The origin of the pilgrimage? 'Oh, pagan sun worship and a chance to mix the gene pools,' was Pat's pragmatic guess.

What was that bird of prey high overhead? Peregrine? Buzzard? No – a golden eagle, a juvenile with white wing patches and broad 'fingers' of outer primary feathers, planing round in effortless circles. We stared up at the young eagle, rapt in admiration of its masterful, careless combination of power and grace, until it was a speck in the sun-hazed sky.

The beautiful and rugged Eglish Valley, sealed in by towering ridges of schist and granite, runs into the heart of the Blue Stack Mountains. The Hamiltons, local landowners, were improving landlords who built handsome two-storey houses along the valley for their tenants. The ruins of the cramped cabins they abandoned lie smothered in grass and heather on the slopes above the Eglish River.

Pat and I chose a rock each and sat absorbing our sandwiches and the view, with ecstatically singing larks for a choir. Then it was up and on, climbing the stony track to a pass between black old turf banks. Up there we halted to take in yet another memorable prospect, a panorama over Lough Eske, laid out in all its serpentine glory, its wooded banks rising through tumbled moorland to the lumpy heights of Croaghconnellagh overlooking the Barnesmore Gap. Beyond rose Barnesmore itself, a pale whale of a mountain harpooned by white wind turbines. It was a view that had me enthralled all the way down to the lake shore.

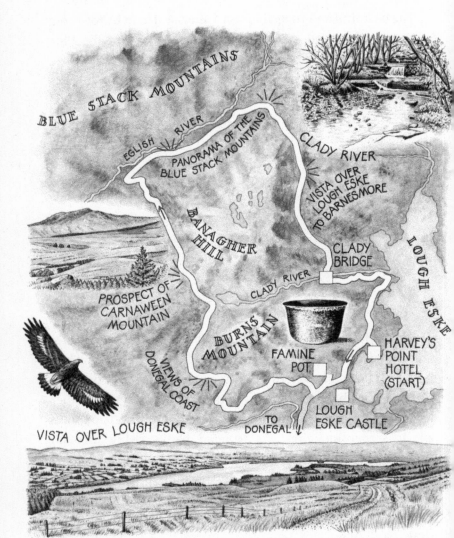

BLUE STACK MOUNTAINS

EGLISH RIVER

PANORAMA OF THE BLUE STACK MOUNTAINS

CLADY RIVER

VISTA OVER LOUGH ESKE TO BARNESMORE

BANAGHER HILL

CLADY BRIDGE

LOUGH ESKE

PROSPECT OF CARNAWEEN MOUNTAIN

CLADY RIVER

BURNS MOUNTAIN

FAMINE POT

HARVEY'S POINT HOTEL (START)

VIEWS OF DONEGAL COAST

LOUGH ESKE CASTLE

TO DONEGAL

VISTA OVER LOUGH ESKE

BURNS MT. & BANAGHER HILL CIRCUIT
BLUE STACK MOUNTAINS, CO. DONEGAL

WAY TO GO

MAP: OS of Ireland 1:50,000 Discovery 11.

TRAVEL:

Bus (www.buseireann.ie) to Donegal town, then taxi (Michael Gallagher, 087-417-6600).

Road: From Donegal Town, N15 Letterkenny road; Harvey's Point Hotel signed left in 1 mile; follow to Harvey's Point Hotel (OSI ref. G 966831).

WALK DIRECTIONS: Left from Harvey's Point. At T-junction, turn right and cross road to see Famine Pot in stone shed. Return to T-junction; keep ahead; right opposite Lough Eske Castle gate, up lane for 2 miles. At 5-way split at summit of road (938827), with 3 gates in view, take middle track (ungated; uphill) for 2 miles. Down at T-junction of tracks (932857), left to metal gate and tarmac road (928860). Forward downhill for 100 yards; sharp right (Blue Stack Way 'walking man'/WM fingerpost) along road. Follow WM for 3½ miles, over pass and down to road (959848). Right (WM) for ⅓ mile; cross Clady Bridge; left (WM) on lane to Harvey's Point.

LENGTH: 10 miles: allow 4–5 hours.

GRADE: Moderate

CONDITIONS: Good tracks, roads.

DON'T MISS:

- Famine Pot
- golden eagles of Eglish Valley (if they're there)
- view over Lough Eske from the pass

REFRESHMENTS / ACCOMMODATION: Harvey's Point Hotel (see below) – warm welcoming, efficient, upmarket, fabulous food.

INFORMATION:

Donegal Tourist Office: The Quay, Donegal; 074-972-1148; www.donegaldirect.ie; www.irelandnorthwest.ie.

Guided walks with Pat Murphy: arrange through Harvey's Point Hotel, Lough Eske, Co Donegal; 074-972-2208; www.harveyspoint.com.

43

CASTLE ARCHDALE AND WHITE ISLAND, CO FERMANAGH

O N A LOVELY SUMMER morning the White Island ferry, zooming across the glassy waters of Lower Lough Erne from Castle Archdale marina, had me landed on the tree-encircled island in somewhat less than a jiffy.

The wartime roar of Sunderland and Catalina flying boats, the suck and hiss as they took off from the lake, the thump and splash as they set down – none of these disturbed the stony staring of the eight watchers of White Island, who had been guarding their islet off Castle Archdale for at least 1,000 years when war came to County Fermanagh in 1941. Today, exploring the ruined church and the enigmatic figures ranked along its wall, I felt that frisson one experiences in the presence of ancient likenesses of the human form.

Who or what had that Dark Ages sculptor been trying to represent? He certainly carved a saucy sheela-na-gig, legs akimbo, who now flashes her monkey grin at one end of the line. The other end is closed by a sulky face. But what of those others in between? Round-eyed, bearing blank expressions and holding mysterious, weather-blurred objects . . . Were these a saintly scribe, a bishop, St David singing with a harp? Two versions of Christ, one banging the heads of two gryphons together, the other a curly-haired warrior with round shield and stabbing sword? Or did their creator have something altogether different in mind when he set to with his chisel on the quartzite slabs he'd smoothed? One stone he left with only the ghostly outline of a figure. What prevented him finishing his great series – sickness, an enemy raid, death? I sat on the landing stage and waited for the ferry back to Castle Archdale with a head full of speculation.

A World War Two heritage trail loops round the headland where in 1615 the 'planter' John Archdale, fresh over in Ulster from Suffolk, built a fortified stronghold. The castle is long gone, but its walled courtyard holds a fascinating wartime exhibition. Lough Erne was perfectly placed (once a secret deal over airspace had been struck with the Republic) for reconnaissance and U-boat hunting trips out into the Atlantic, and the wooded peninsula became home to thousands of youngsters from many corners of the world. I learned with admiration of those flyers from Britain, Canada and the US, their stolid courage on the job, and the high jinks they got up to back at base in order to let off steam.

Walking the trail, I crossed beautiful woodland where the horse chestnuts were displaying the faded remnants of pink and white candle flowers. Under the trees crouched the shapes of fuel and ammunition stores smothered under moss and ivy, as overgrown and ancient-looking as Stone Age huts. It was strange to walk with so many ghosts – down on the marina with its big white beacon and memorial stone to wartime crash victims, and out along the 'Burma Road', a jungly path cut through the forest to reach the isolated explosives dumps. These days a caravan park covers the maintenance apron where the flying boats were repaired, and bluebells carpet the glade where Canadian aircrew once roomed in Nissen huts that were nicknamed 'Skunk Hollow' because their sewers gave out an ineradicable stink. From here the young lads would escape to local bars and dance halls, to laugh and drink and jive and jitterbug like hell.

Down on the lake path the view was of low hills reflected in wide water. Coots honked stridently from the reed beds. A swan came in from the open lake, sawing its wings, as white and lumbering as a Sunderland flying boat. It skated along the water, kicking up a bow wave. A shiver of folding wings, a shake of the neck, and it was sailing serenely to shore. All seemed right with the world under the blue Fermanagh sky; and as I passed ponds shimmering with water boatmen and turned back towards the Courtyard Centre, I could only hope that those young Air Force men and women, at war and far from home, had snatched some precious moments such as these.

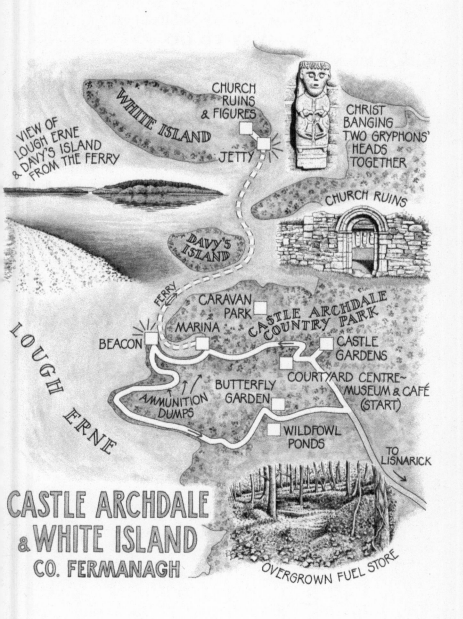

WHITE ISLAND

CHURCH RUINS & FIGURES

VIEW OF LOUGH ERNE & DAVY'S ISLAND FROM THE FERRY

JETTY

CHRIST BANGING TWO GRYPHONS' HEADS TOGETHER

CHURCH RUINS

DAVY'S ISLAND

FERRY

CARAVAN PARK

CASTLE ARCHDALE COUNTRY PARK

MARINA

CASTLE GARDENS

BEACON

COURTYARD CENTRE-MUSEUM & CAFÉ (START)

AMMUNITION DUMPS

BUTTERFLY GARDEN

LOUGH ERNE

WILDFOWL PONDS

TO LISNARICK

CASTLE ARCHDALE & WHITE ISLAND CO. FERMANAGH

OVERGROWN FUEL STORE

WAY TO GO

MAP: OS of Northern Ireland 1:50,000 Discoverer 17; downloadable maps/instructions at www.walkni.com.

TRAVEL:

Rail/bus (integrated website – www.nirailways.co.uk): Ulsterbus 194 (Pettigo-Enniskillen) to Lisnarick (1 mile).

Road: Signed off B82/B72 at Lisnarick (postcode BT94 1PP).

WALK DIRECTIONS: (World War Two Heritage Trail marked with numbered posts): From Courtyard Centre descend steps to car park; sharp left past 'No Entry' sign on path through trees. Follow 'Woodland Walk' signs to roadway. Left for 30 yards; right to marina. Left to beacon; left along shore path; bear right at yellow marker, continue on cycle track. At another yellow marker, right to shore path. Follow it through Skunk Hollow car park. Follow 'Butterfly Garden' past pond, butterfly garden and deer enclosure. Dogleg right and left to gate at drive (don't go through!). Left along path; right to castle gardens.

LENGTH: 2½ miles: allow 1–2 hours.

GRADE: Easy

DON'T MISS:
• World War Two exhibition
• White Island
• butterfly garden

REFRESHMENTS: Castle Archdale Tearoom.

INFORMATION:

White Island ferry 028-6862-1892: July–August daily, Sept weekends.

Castle Archdale Visitor Centre: 028-6862-1588; www.ni-environment.gov.uk/places_to_visit. . ./parks/archdale.htm.

Guide books/leaflets: available at Visitor Centre.

Other information: www.discovernorthernireland.com.

44

SLIEVE GULLION, CO ARMAGH

'EVER SMELT PINE NEEDLES properly?' enquired Ron Murray, reaching out to pluck a spiny sprig as we strolled the Forest Drive along the southern flank of Slieve Gullion. 'Crush 'em like this between your finger and thumb.' I suited action to words, and sniffed deeply. A spicy blast of orange as pungent as a marmalade factory. Now why had I never noticed that before?

Until recently Ron served as officer for the Ring of Gullion Area of Outstanding Natural Beauty. When you're out and about with someone so observant and experienced, all five senses get a re-bore. Birds, rocks, landforms, farming practices, local history, ancient monuments – all came alive for me during this walk over the big dark hump of Slieve Gullion, centrepiece of a remarkable volcanic landscape set in the green farmlands of South Armagh. Surprisingly few people – walkers or others – venture into the countryside south-west of Newry to climb the mountain and savour for themselves one of the most spectacular high-level views in Ireland.

Rowan and silver birch were coming into leaf all along the sides of Slieve Gullion. We left the trees and turned aside to climb, short and sharp, to the southern peak of the mountain. Smoking rainstorms whirled djinn-like across the lower lands as we pulled to a halt by the stony cairn and turned for a proper appreciation of the whole grand panorama.

If you can see one mile, you can see well over 100 from the summit of Slieve Gullion. In the east Carlingford Lough, running north-east to Slieve Donard and the hummocky backbone of the Mountains of Mourne. Northwards, the tumbled hills of Antrim, with the block-head of Slemish some 50 miles off. North-west the billowy heave and roll of the Sperrins, a gleam of Lough Neagh at their feet. South-west the green-and-brown mat of Monaghan and Cavan, unrolling into the Midland plain. And down in the south, diminutive, unmistakable and as pale as tin cut-outs, the hills of Wicklow more than 60 miles away.

Until I was surfeited with this gigantic panorama, the Ring of Gullion itself had to play second fiddle. It was a series of unimaginably powerful subterranean convulsions some 60 million years ago which caused the ancient and original Slieve Gullion volcano to collapse into the great chamber that lay beneath it, sending a ripple of molten rock outwards like a stone thrown in a pond. The circular ridge solidified, then weathered over ages into the guardian hills of the Ring, a ten-mile-wide circle of craggy mini-mountains encircling Slieve Gullion like courtiers round a king.

I turned away from the breathtaking prospect at last, to find Ron beckoning like a Beatrix Potter dormouse from a little low doorway of stone set deep into the side of the cairn. On hands and knees I followed him inside, to find a chamber walled with stones neatly shaped and fitted. A neolithic passage grave under a Bronze Age cairn, say the archaeologists. Not at all, retort the romantics. Here is the house of the Cailleach Beara, the unspeakably wicked witch who turned mighty Fionn MacCumhaill into the feeblest of old men in the time it took him to dive into the Lake of Sorrows to retrieve her golden ring. Of course, the fact she'd disguised herself as a beautiful, shapely young maiden in distress had nothing to do with Fionn's recklessness.

Ron and I strode the windy summit ridge past the Lake of Sorrows. What on earth was a millstone doing up here, half in and half out of the water? 'Oh, a miller pinched it from the Cailleach Beara's house,' said Ron, 'but it brought him such bad luck that he decided to put it back. When his donkey had got it this far, the poor thing fell down dead. So that's where it stayed from then on. No one quite fancies moving it . . .'

SLIEVE GULLION
CO. ARMAGH

CAM LOUGH

SLIEVE GULLION

AIM FOR
WHITE HOUSE

RON MURRAY
WITH AN OLD WAYMARK

KILLEVY
OLD CHURCH

CLONLUM
CHAMBERED
GRAVE

ST. BLINE'S
HOLY WELL

NORTH
CAIRN

GREAT VIEW
WEST FROM PICNIC SHELTER

LAKE OF SORROWS

CLONLUM
CAIRN TOMB

TURN RIGHT UPHILL
AT WHITE POST

WONDERFUL
360° VIEWS

SLIEVE GULLION

SOUTH
CAIRN
(CAILLEACH
BEARA'S HOUSE)

TO NEWRY
B113

CAR
PARK
WITH
PICNIC BENCH

CAR PARK
(START & FINISH)

COURTYARD CENTRE

NICE CUPPA!

CHRISTOPHER AT
CAILLEACH BEARA'S
HOUSE

LAKE OF SORROWS

DON'T... DIVE IN
...TALK TO STRANGE MAIDENS
...OR MOVE THE MILLSTONE!

WAY TO GO

MAP: OS of Northern Ireland 1:50,000 Discoverer Series Sheet 29.

TRAVEL:

Bus: Service 43 (Newry–Forkhill) to Forest Park entrance.

Road: N1/A1 Dublin–Newry; B113 ('Forkhill'); in 3½ miles, right ('Slieve Gullion Forest Park') to car park.

WALK DIRECTIONS: (Ring of Gullion Way/RGW blue arrows): From top left corner of car park (OS ref J 040196), left up path through trees. In ¼ mile join Forest Drive (038191), up slope, then level, for ¼ mile to RGW post on left (035190). Right up drive, past metal barrier; left uphill for 1½ miles to car park (018200). Beyond picnic table, right at white post, steeply uphill to South Cairn on Slieve Gullion summit (025203).

Walk past Lake of Sorrows to North Cairn (021211); then aim north for Sturgan Mountain (left of Cam Lough), then white house between you and lake. Path divides by grassy 'lawn' with boulder beyond; right here, aiming for house. Through gate, down to road (025230). Right along road for 3 miles, passing Killevy Old Church (040221) and Clonlum Cairn (047206), to northern entrance to Slieve Gullion Forest Park (046199). Right to car park.

LENGTH: 8 miles.

GRADE: Moderate

CONDITIONS: Can be muddy.

DON'T MISS:
• Cailleach Beara's house
• Lake of Sorrows and enchanted millstone
• sensational views from Slieve Gullion

REFRESHMENTS: Slieve Gullion Courtyard Centre.

INFORMATION:

Tourist Office: Newry Town Hall (00-44-2830-268877).

Slieve Gullion Courtyard Center (02830-849220); http://www.discovernorthernireland.com/Slieve-Gullion-Courtyard-Killeavy-Newry-P3079.

45

MOUNT STEWART AND STRANGFORD LOUGH, CO DOWN

'**Y**OU'VE GOT TO DO it,' urged David Thompson, National Trust warden on Strangford Lough, over the phone. 'You'll kick yourself if you don't!'

That kind of advice needs to be heeded – which is why Jane and I found ourselves on a blowy afternoon, rubber boots on and biblical-looking wooden staves in hand, squelching in David's company from the gates of Mount Stewart out across the muddy bed of Strangford Lough towards the distant hump of Chapel Island.

Earlier in the day the three of us had been lucky enough to be shown over the wonderful Mount Stewart gardens by the Head Gardener, Philip Rollinson. There is a man with a profound feeling for trees and plants, a prerequisite for looking after gardens as exotic – and as quixotic – as those laid out by Edith, Lady Londonderry from 1921 onwards around her Mount Stewart residence.

Edith, wife of the 7th Marquess of Londonderry, was a serious plantswoman, but she was also a socialite, a heavyweight political hostess, a pioneer pilot, and a great lover of light and laughter. She abhorred Mount Stewart on her first visit there: 'I thought the house and surroundings were the dampest, darkest and saddest place I had ever stayed in.' How she worked to turn it all around! She devised Italian and Spanish gardens, lake walks and lily woods, and a sea garden with date palms and rhododendrons to keep at bay the eternal salt winds off the tidal lough. And she laid out the craziest of promenades, a Dodo Terrace bristling with stone carvings representing members of her 'Ark Club' of friends and colleagues – apes with cloven hooves, frogs and hedgehogs, and the dyspeptic-looking dodos themselves.

Above the lake we climbed a bank to Tir na n'Og, the walled mausoleum where Edith and her husband lie buried in elaborate sarcophagi. A milk-white stag in statue form roams the lawns beyond, symbol of hope and fantasy.

From the slender octagonal Temple of the Winds on its knoll we looked out across Strangford Lough. The tremulous *pik! pik!* of oystercatchers came up from the ebbing tideline where Chapel Island lay low and dark. 'Time to go,' decided David Thompson.

Who built the chapel out in the sea lough? History is silent, but it was probably a hermit monk from Movilla Abbey near Newtownards, some seeker after solitude. As we splashed and skidded through bladderweed hanks and drifts of cockle shells, I pictured him, a holy crazy with fishbones in his beard and a furnace for a spirit, trudging barefoot across the mud to the lonely tidal island to eke out a harsh existence and excoriate body and soul.

Pale-bellied brent geese were feeding on the wide mudflats, with a most beautiful skyline as a backdrop – Slieve Croob's long back rising towards the south-west, and the multiple humps of the Mourne Mountains silhouetted down in the south against a lemon and silver sky, smeared over with an iridescence of petrol pink and blue.

We came ashore on Chapel Island across a beach of black and orange pebbles. A snipe leaped up from the grass and dashed zigzagging away with a whirr of sickle-shaped wings. Up on the shaggy spine of the island we trod south, coming quite suddenly on the sunken foundations of the chapel. Oyster shells and cuttlebones lay like offerings on the shaped stones. 'Whoever lived here wouldn't have starved, that's for sure,' David said. 'Oysters, shellfish, salmon; see the stone walls of the fish trap in the mud down there? Then the wild plants,' – he swept a hand across island and distant shore – 'sorrel, dulse, samphire, carrageen moss, sea beet. He might have been a wild man, but he wouldn't have been a hungry one.'

The tide had slackened, and was beginning to gurgle back in through distant sandbanks further out in the lough. We shook ourselves back to reality and stepped down on to the mud. Plodding to shore in the half light I paused and looked back beyond Chapel Island, where the sun was slipping towards the upheld arms of the Mournes through a sky as red and raging as any fiery furnace.

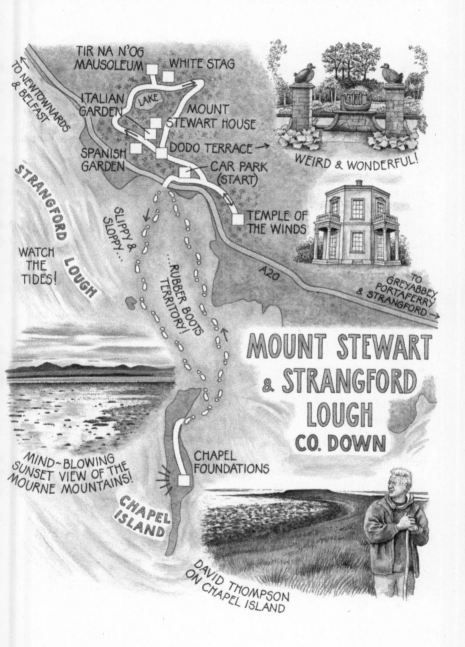

TIR NA N'OG MAUSOLEUM

WHITE STAG

ITALIAN GARDEN

LAKE

MOUNT STEWART HOUSE

TO NEWTOWNARDS & BELFAST

SPANISH GARDEN

DODO TERRACE →

CAR PARK (START)

WEIRD & WONDERFUL!

STRANGFORD LOUGH

WATCH THE TIDES!

SLIPPY & SLOPPY...

TEMPLE OF THE WINDS

A20

RUBBER BOOTS TERRITORY!

TO GREYABBEY, PORTAFERRY & STRANGFORD

MOUNT STEWART & STRANGFORD LOUGH CO. DOWN

MIND~BLOWING SUNSET VIEW OF THE MOURNE MOUNTAINS!

CHAPEL FOUNDATIONS

CHAPEL ISLAND

DAVID THOMPSON ON CHAPEL ISLAND

WAY TO GO

MAP: OS of Northern Ireland 1:50,000 Discoverer 21; Mount Stewart garden map from NT shop; downloadable map/instructions (highly recommended) at www walkni.com.

TRAVEL:

Rail/bus (integrated website – www.nirailways.co.uk): Ulsterbus 10 (Belfast-Portaferry).

Road: A20 Newtownards–Portaferry.

WALK DIRECTIONS: Make a circuit of the Mount Stewart gardens and grounds then walk out across Strangford Lough at low tide to Chapel Island.

NB Tides and soft sands can make the Strangford Lough section dangerous. Only do this walk as part of a guided group – contact Mount Stewart (see below) or David Thompson (028-4488-1204) for details.

LENGTH: 5 miles: allow 3 hours.

GRADE: Easy

CONDITIONS: Muddy across Strangford Lough – wellingtons/waterproof boots.

DON'T MISS:
- Dodo Terrace
- sensational skies and birds
- chapel remains

REFRESHMENTS: Bay Restaurant, Mount Stewart (024-4278-7805).

INFORMATION:

Newtownards Tourist Office: Regent Street (02891-826846).

www.discovernorthernireland.com.

Mount Stewart (National Trust): 024-4278-8387; www.nationaltrust.org.uk.

Guide books/leaflets: From NT shop.

46

GLENARIFF, CO ANTRIM

GLENARIFF, 'QUEEN OF THE Antrim Glens', lay stroked by early mist. From the high perch of Glenariff Forest Park, the views that Jane and I had of the upthrust cliffs of the glen seemed softened and toned down. But as the summer morning broadened and the sun came through, the hard purple and slate hues of the naked rock reinstated themselves.

The nine Glens of Antrim are harsh country. Glenariff, largest and deepest of all, is no exception. Like its neighbouring clefts, bleak moorland tops Glenariff. Ancient woodland clothes its flanks, and rivers and springs cut down through the basalt that formed it some 60 million years ago, the seaward pouring of a gigantic outflow of lava. Ice Age glaciers gouged Glenariff deep and narrow, and tumbling waterfalls and cataracts continue the scouring process today. Four Forest Trails show walkers a number of aspects of Glenariff, and this morning Jane and I were aiming to link up the longer of the walks, the Waterfall Walk and the Scenic Trail, to taste the cream of this superb landscape.

Blue tits gave out a thin, clockwork *pzzit! pzzit!* and chaffinches their explosive run-and-hurl-the-ball songs as we descended the path towards the Glenariff River, whose faint roar came up from far below. Down there in the leafy half light we crossed Rainbow Bridge to explore the damp cleft beyond, every crevice packed and dripping with luxuriant moss cushions,

231

jointed horsetails and creamy fungi sucking moisture from rotting logs. 'Bryophytes,' murmured Jane the botany graduate, parting the mosses round a sodden tree stump to reveal fleshy dark green leaves like a miniature tropical forest. 'They need a *lot* of water . . .'

The Waterfall Walk led us down wooden stairs and along teetery walkways, winding deeper into the gorge cut by the Glenariff River. At one moment the path ran beside the river; the next it had leaped 50 feet above it and was catwalking along the wall of the cleft. Zigzagging back down, we crossed a bridge and turned to enjoy a spectacular sight: the double cascade of Ess-na-Larach, the Mare's Fall, tumbling like a swishing horse's tail 50 feet into a smoking pool, then sluicing over rocks almost as far again to hiss into the bed of the gorge.

Just above the confluence of the Glenariff and Inver Rivers is the second of the glen's breathtaking waterfalls, Ess-na-Crub, the Fall of the Hooves – another equine inspiration, perhaps drawn from the thunderous noise of the water. We drank a cup of tea in the Laragh Lodge café, looking out through the trees towards Ess-na-Crub.

'The thing I like about that view,' said the owner, peering out and grinning as though savouring it for the first time, 'is it changes all the time. In a few months those leaves will be on fire; then they'll drop and we'll be able to see the fall properly; and then the snow will be down and it'll be different again.'

We turned aside to see the Fall of the Hooves at close quarters, and then commenced a long back-and-forth climb through the forest to the lip of the glen. Up there the moorland lay silent under strong sunlight. The upper falls of the Inver River came crashing over a basalt lip high on the skyline. Turning down the homeward path we saw the whole of Glenariff stretched out ahead, purple cliffs on high, wooded slopes sweeping down to a far-off glimpse of the sea in Red Bay, where a solitary fishing boat rocked at ease in the hazy summer afternoon.

TO BALLYMENA

RAINBOW BRIDGE

ESS~NA~LARACH WATERFALL

LARAGH LODGE CAFE

EXCELLENT PIT STOP!

TO WATERFOOT

GLENARIFF RIVER

ESS~NA~CRUB WATERFALL

EXCITING WALKWAYS & LADDERS!

CAR PARK (START & FINISH)

VISITOR CENTRE & CAFE

INVER RIVER

GARDEN HUTS

SCENIC TRAIL

BEAR RIGHT OFF SCENIC TRAIL

KEEP EYES & EARS PEELED FOR DEER & FOREST BIRDS

VIEWS OVER GLENARIFF

GLENARIFF RIVER WALKWAY

WONDERFUL VIEW TO RED BAY!

IGNORE TRACK TO RIGHT OF HUT

UPPER FALLS OF INVER RIVER

ESS~NA~CRUB WATERFALL

SCENIC TRAIL IN THE FOREST

GLENARIFF, CO. ANTRIM

WAY TO GO

MAP: OS of Northern Ireland 1:50,000 Discoverer 9; downloadable map/instrucions at www.walkni.com, and www.forestserviceni.gov.uk.

TRAVEL:

Bus (www.nirailways.co.uk): Ulsterbus Service 150 (Ballymena–Cushendun) stops at Glenariff Forest Park.

Road: From A2 coast road at Waterfoot, A43 Ballymena road passes Glenariff Forest Park.

WALK DIRECTIONS: From Glenariff Forest Park car park, follow Waterfall Walk/WW signs. At foot of slope, by WW signboard, bear left down path to cross Rainbow Bridge. Track soon doubles back to re-cross bridge and continue along WW. Follow WW to Laragh Lodge tearoom.

Cross Glenariff River and start up track; detour left to see Ess-na-Crub Waterfall; hen on up track. In 100 m fork left to cross Inver River, following Scenic Trail/ST upwards through zigzags and up steps and slopes for 2½ miles to cross upper waters of Inver River. A few 100 m further on, track marked by signboard branches sharply right past hut; ignore this, and continue for ½ mile to where ST crosses downward-sloping track opposite old quarry hopper. Bear right off ST down track; right by building at bottom to reach wooden huts in gardens. Steps behind huts lead up into gardens; bear right ('Viewpoint Walk') to car park.

LENGTH: 5 miles: allow 2½–3 hours.

GRADE: Moderate

CONDITIONS: Many steps; some steep slopes; paths can be slippery.

DON'T MISS:
• Ess-na-Larach Waterfall on Glenariff River
• Ess-na-Crub Waterfall on Inver River
• spectacular falls to left as you cross upper Inver River
• views on way back, down Glenariff to sea

REFRESHMENTS: Glenariff Forest Park Café; Laragh Lodge Restaurant (028-2175-8221).

INFORMATION:

Ballymena Tourist Office: The Braid, Bridge Street; 028-2563-5900; www.discovernorthernireland.com.

Trail leaflets from Glenariff Forest Park Visitor Centre; trail boards near car park.

47

CROAGHAN, CO ANTRIM

THE SKY OVER COUNTY Antrim was a slate grey bar pressing down on the horizon. The forest steamed. Swirling curls of mist drifted across moor and mountain. The peak of Croaghan stood wrapped in silvery backlit cloud. Jane and I sat in the car at Altarichard as rain spattered the windows, and wondered what to do. Give up now? Have a go and hang the weather? Well – let's do the walk back to front, starting in the forest. The trees'll give us a bit of shelter, and Croaghan will have a chance to kick off the cloud blankets before we get there.

Rain bounced off our noses and shoulders. The forest ran with water. Every channel was a bubbling, noisy millrace under brilliant green mats of sphagnum. Fly agaric fungi raised their toxic heads under the conifers, the rim of each shining scarlet cap nibbled into lace. What could eat a fly agaric without tripping out into insanity and death? Wow, man. There must be some highly psychedelic insects in the Antrim forests.

'A five-star wet forest, half land and half water,' murmured Jane, picking blueberries beside the track. Each bush was hung with gleaming fruit, a raindrop pendulous from every berry. Gradually the rain slackened, and patches of blue began to spread like celestial butter across the western sky. After the deluge, the Ugly Bugs

236

Ball. Heather and grass suddenly crawled with life: spiders with hugely swollen white abdomens, steel-blue thrips with feathery wings, fat buttery caterpillars, a lumbering black oil beetle as long as the top joint of my thumb. A small copper butterfly, sensing the sun about to emerge, opened wings of burnt orange vividly spotted with patches of deep charcoal grey.

Out in the open we splashed and slid through patches of sodden turf and heather clumps pearled with moisture, then turned in among the trees once more. Walking north on the edge of Corvarrive, a wonderful view opened out ahead across the Antrim farmlands to the domed green head of Knocklayd streaked with ancient erosion channels, and beyond the mountain the white and black cliffs of Rathlin Island out at sea a dozen miles off.

A last long stretch through spruce, up to the knees in sucking bog, the fallen boughs draped with mats of moss like shaggy green yaks, goldcrests calling *seep-seep* from the topmost sprigs. Then out on to the open hillside, forging up the north flank of Croaghan on a well-beaten path trickling with water, through heather bristly with old dried sprouts of bog asphodel. In clear sky on the top of Croaghan, a blasting wind and a mighty view. To the north behind the grey hummock of Knocklayd and its pimple of a summit cairn, the ghost of Rathlin sliding in and out of the grey and white slabs of rain pounding the coast. In the south a forest of wind turbines semaphoring

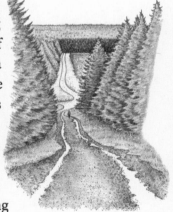

beyond Slieveanorra. And to the west a heavenly prospect of sunlit plains, with more rain making ready to sweep in over the border from the Sperrin Hills in cloudy Tyrone.

As we squelched down over the moor on the homeward path, I all but trod on a beautifully camouflaged frog, as olive-coloured and gleaming as the mud he crouched in. One easy, remarkable jump took him ten frog-lengths away into a patch of sphagnum. There he squatted, gulping rhythmically, waiting with all the monumental patience of nature for me to move on out of his sphere.

JANE & CROAGHAN

MOYLE WAY
GOES AHEAD~
BUT KEEP LEFT!

CROAGHAN
CO. ANTRIM

VERY BOGGY
ALONG HERE!

FLY AGARIC
FUNGI

SUPERB PANORAMA
OF KNOCKLAYD

CROAGHAN

SEA VIEWS TO
RATHLIN ISLAND

BLUE ROUTE
GOES LEFT~ BUT
KEEP AHEAD!

WET MOORLAND

SEDGY
GROUND!

Glenshesk River

TO
MAGHERAHONEY
& BALLYMENA

(START &
FINISH)

ALTARICHARD
CAR PARK

FOREST ROAD

PANORAMA OF KNOCKLAYD

239

WAY TO GO

MAP: OS of Northern Ireland 1:50,000 Discoverer 5; downloadable map/instructions (highly recommended) at www.walkni.com.

TRAVEL:

A44 Ballymena towards Ballycastle; in 17 miles, right to Magherahoney; left across Bush River, first right, then first left (brown 'Orra Scenic Route' signs); Altarichard car park is on left in 1½ miles.

WALK DIRECTIONS: *NB The walk as recommended here follows the official Croaghan loop **in reverse***; *direction arrows are on reverse of guide posts!* From car park (OSNI ref D 124293), right along road, round two bends; take first forest road on left (past metal gate). In 300 m it doglegs right (132297), then left (red arrows/RA, and blue arrows/BA); then runs NNW for ⅔ mile to T-junction (129306). Left (RA, BA) for 100 m (very boggy!) to post (RA, BA); right over stile to post; left for 200 m along forest edge; right (126306; RA, BA) into forest. In 200 m, left (RA, BA) up forest road. In 150 m, Blue Route turns left towards Croaghan mountain (124308; BA), but continue ahead. In 1⅓ miles, Moyle Way (MW) comes in from grassy path ahead (129327; yellow arrows); follow forest road uphill to left, and on for ½ mile. Turn left off Moyle Way (124331; RA) up side road. Where road ends, bear left (RA) up grassy ride (very boggy!) to edge of trees (117316; RA). Follow posts uphill across moorland to summit of Croaghan (118308); aim for car park 1 mile away.

LENGTH: 6 miles: allow 3 hours.

GRADE: Easy/Moderate

CONDITIONS: Very boggy in parts after rain; wellingtons or waterproof boots!

DON'T MISS:
- views of Knocklayd and Rathlin Island
- views from Croaghan

REFRESHMENTS: None en route – take a picnic.

INFORMATION:

Tourist Office: Mary Street, Ballycastle; 028/048-2076-2024; www.causeway coastandglens.com; www.discovernorthernireland.com.

Guide to Walking Causeway Coast & Glens from TICs.

48

DOWNHILL ESTATE AND BENONE STRAND, CO DERRY

FREDERICK HERVEY, 4TH EARL of Bristol, Bishop of Londonderry from 1768–1803, was a remarkably broad-minded man. In that intolerant era of the Penal Laws, the Bishop allowed the local priest to celebrate Mass in the Mussenden Temple, one of the follies he erected around his preposterously extravagant Downhill Estate on the cliffs outside Castlerock. Hervey was also fabulously red-blooded and eccentric, fond of his wine and the ladies, addicted to foreign travel and art collecting, apt to have himself borne around in a palanquin and to drop spaghetti on the heads of pilgrims passing below his balcony in Rome.

Jane and I entered Downhill on a brisk windy morning under the knowing grins of the ounces or mythic lynx-like beasts – superbly restored recently – that guard the estate's so-called 'Lion Gate'. Beyond the partly replanted Walled Garden we found the Bishop's enormous Palace of Downhill in poignant ruin, its grand fireplaces hollow and stark, its windows blank, state rooms carpeted with grass and open to the sky. In the heyday of Downhill this incredible centre of luxury high on the cliffs had an entrance facade flanked by Corinthian pilasters, with a double stair leading to the door. There was a State Dining Room, a State Drawing Room, and a two-storey gallery for the Bishop's superb art collection, all covered by a magnificent dome. Facade and double stair still stand, but now the interior walls, once beautified with exquisite plasterwork, are sealed with functional Ministry-of-Works concrete, the elaborate mosaics are gone from the chimney breasts, and buttercups and clover have taken the place of Wilton and Axminster. It's a strange, uncanny and altogether haunting atmosphere in the empty shell of the Palace of Downhill.

Down on the brink of the basalt cliffs beside the domed Mussenden Temple, we looked out on a most sensational view: the sea shallows creaming on seven clear miles of sand that ran west in a gentle curve towards the mouth of Lough Foyle, with the clouded hills of 'dark Inishowen' beckoning from far-off Donegal.

That proved a quite irresistible call. Down on the strand we pushed into the wind. Waves hissed on the tideline, sand particles scudded by. Surfers rode the waves like water demons. The black and green rampart of the cliffs was cut vertically by white strings of waterfalls, the falling cascades blown to rags in mid-plummet. All this vigour and movement whipped us onwards to where the preserved sand dunes of Umbra rose between strand and cliff foot. A complete change of tempo here, sheltered among the sandhills, down on our hands and knees among pyramidal orchids of blazing crimson, yellow kidney vetch, lady's bedstraw sacred to the Virgin Mary, and tall spikes of common spotted orchids of such a seductive milky pink and blue it was all I could do not to take a surreptitious lick at them.

Lying prone in the dunes, looking back through a screen of marram grass and clovers, we saw the dark pepperpot shape of the temple on the brink of Downhill cliff. Had the bold Bishop of Londonderry kept a mistress in there, as stories say? I rather hoped he had, and his palanquin and spaghetti-tureen, too.

Sand yachts were scudding along Benone Strand, chased by the most diminutive of tiddly tiny terriers. The Bishop of Londonderry in his red and raging guise could have swallowed the puppy with one gulp. In another mood he might have made it a curate, or given it the run of the palace Axminsters. What a splendid fellow, for those on the right side of him.

WAY TO GO

MAP: OS of Northern Ireland 1:50,000 Discoverer 04; downloadable map/instructions (highly recommended) at www.walkni.com.

TRAVEL:

Rail/bus (integrated website – www.nirailways.co.uk): Rail to Castlerock (½ mile). Ulsterbus service 134.

Road: Downhill Estate is on A2 between Castlerock and Downhill Strand.

WALK DIRECTIONS: From Lion Gate car park (OS of NI ref C 757357), explore the Walled Garden, then Downhill Palace ruin, then Mussenden Temple (758362). Return anti-clockwise along the cliff. From Lion Gate cross A2 (take care!); turn right downhill beside the road along pavement. There's a short stretch with no pavement before you reach the foot of the hill. Turn right under the railway, then left along Downhill Strand. After 1¼ miles, where a river leaves the dunes, look left for Ulster Wildlife Trust's Umbra Dunes notice (732359). Follow the fence through dunes, looking over into Umbra Dunes Reserve, before descending on to Benone Strand. Continue to Benone (717362 – lavatories, Visitor Centre, sometimes ice-cream vans). Return along the beach and A2 to Lion Gate car park.

LENGTH: 6 miles: allow 2–3 hours.

GRADE: Easy

CONDITIONS: Good paths, firm sands.

DON'T MISS:
● the strange ruins of Downhill Palace
● Mussenden Temple on the cliff edge
● flowery delights of Umbra dunes

REFRESHMENTS: Pretty Crafty Studio (signed across A2 from Lion Gate) is a great place for tea and cakes; or take a picnic on the beach.

INFORMATION:

Tourist Office: Railway Road, Coleraine; 028-7034-4723; www.discovernorthernireland.com.

Downhill (NT): 028-2073-1582; www.nationaltrust.org.uk.

Umbra Dunes (Ulster Wildlife Trust):

www.ulsterwildlifetrust.org/nature+reserves/Umbra.

49

CARNTOGHER MOUNTAIN, NEAR MAGHERA, CO DERRY

THEY HAD ALL THE flags out in Swatragh for the Derry County Senior Hurling Final. 'Horse it into them, Swa!' urged a big hand-painted banner by the roadside. Sadly, it was Dungiven who horsed it into Swatragh that particular afternoon, 0-12 to 0-8. But I don't suppose the men of Swa ever hold back too much. Learning your hurling in the shadow of Carntogher would be an inspiration to anyone, the long sloping shoulder of mountain lying at your back like the mother of all goalies, or the great hurler Cúchulainn himself.

Down in the glen of the Altkeeran River all was sedgy, the fields dotted with rushes and the streamsides with scrub trees where long-tailed tits went *pit-peet*-ing among the silver birches. The old coach road along the glen gave firm footing through the turf which squelched and bounced under every incautious step. Streams ran orange from the iron minerals of the mountain, up whose green flank Jane and I turned to climb towards the Snout of the Cairn. The views widened the higher we went – the hard humpy outline of Slemish due east in Antrim, the neat grouping of Mourne peaks 60 miles off on County Down's south-easterly skyline, and nearer at hand the rolling bulk of the Sperrin Hills across in Tyrone.

Pink conquistador helmets of lousewort clashed with virulent red sphagnum in the banks of the tumbled wall we were following. It lifted us to the shoulder of the mountain, and a track where we met our first and only walkers of the day, two men of a local townland who pointed out Slieve Gallion ten miles to the south ('a Derry mountain, despite what you might hear') with great precision and pride. 'I've walked this path since I was a boy,' said one, 'and by God I will do it till the day that I die!'

Up at the Snout of the Cairn, Shane's Leaps lay just off the path – three innocuous-looking rocks. Did that dashing and irrepressible 18th-century rapparee Shane 'Crossagh' O'Mullan, the scar-faced outlaw whom all the ladies sighed for, really spring lightly from one to the next in the act of outwitting the lumbering English soldiery? So tales tell us, and how we like to picture such derring-do. Much more shadowed and sombre are the images the skull cinema brings up at the Emigrants' Cairn, where the heart-stopping view to the hills of Donegal was the last that those walking over the mountains to the ships in Lough Foyle took away with them to 'far Amerikay'.

Back across the slopes of Carntogher we went, following the boggiest of upland tracks, half peat and half puddle, past black heaps of iron-mining spoil to the top of the ridge and another most tremendous westward view, across the silver fishtail of Lough Foyle, on beyond the pale humps of Barnesmore and the Blue Stacks to the jagged spine of Errigal out at the edge of sight in western Donegal. Between Errigal and Mourne there cannot be fewer than 100 miles. All Northern Ireland lay spread out for us, and we lingered long over this extraordinary feast.

On the way down we passed a Bronze Age cist grave, carefully labelled 'Tuama ón Ré Chré Umha'. Now that might just mean 'the old tomb from the Bronze Age', but there was something about the little dark hole in the bank, slab-lined and secretive, that simply invited a taller and wilder tale. But no one was there to tell it to us today.

SENSATIONAL VIEWS TO DONEGAL!

PANORAMA OF CARNTOGHER MOUNTAIN

CARNTOGHER

GREAT VIEWS TO ALL QUARTERS!

RED ARROW

DETOUR LEFT

STAR MOSSES

CIST GRAVE

WHAT'S THE STORY..?

RED ARROW

SHANE'S LEAPS

FOLLOW OLD WALL UPHILL

TURN RIGHT ALONG ROAD

TUAMA ÓN RÉ CHRÉ UMHA (CIST GRAVE)

EMIGRANTS' CAIRN

LOVELY WATERFALL

LEFT BY CYLINDRICAL GATEPOST

CARNTOGHER MOUNTAIN TRAIL START POINT & MAP

ORANGE STREAMS!

ALTKEERAN RIVER

CAR PARK

TO MAGHERA

MOUNTAIN TRACK

CARNTOGHER MOUNTAIN
NEAR MAGHERA, CO. DERRY

WAY TO GO

MAPS: OS of Northern Ireland 1:50,000 Discoverer 8; downloadable map/instructions (highly recommended) at http://www.walkni.com/d/walks/319/Carntogher_History_Trail.pdf; map of trail at car park.

TRAVEL:

Bus (integrated website – www.nirailways.co.uk): Ulsterbus to Maghera (3 miles) or Swatragh (3½ miles).

Road: A29 (Coleraine–Maghera); minor roads to parking place by ruined cottage at Tullykeeran Bridge (OSNI ref C 819045).

WALK DIRECTIONS: (red trail): Continue along road. 100 m beyond 3rd bridge, left over stile by cylindrical gatepost (red/blue arrows); follow track for ½ mile into Altkeeran Glen (805407 approx). Turn right up path by tumbledown wall (red/blue arrows on posts). In ½ mile, stony track crosses path (800058 approx); left (red arrow) to Snout of the Cairn viewpoint at Emigrants' Cairn and Shane's Leap rocks (796058).

Retrace steps for 50 yards; left at post (red arrow) along grassy track to marker post on saddle of ground; walk 400 yards left here to ridge for great view over Lough Foyle and Donegal hills; return to marker post. Continue downhill along track for 2 miles, past cist grave (824061), through gates, down to road (823055). Right (red arrow) for 2 miles to car park.

LENGTH: 5½ miles: allow 3 hours.

GRADE: Moderate

CONDITIONS: Mountain hike on hill tracks – wear boots, hill-walking gear. Take binoculars for spotting waymark posts! Very boggy between Snout of the Cairn and Lough Foyle viewpoint.

DON'T MISS:
- view from Emigrants' Cairn and Shane's Leap Rocks
- view over Lough Foyle from ridge
- 'Tuama ón Ré Chré Umha' – cist grave

REFRESHMENTS: Rafters Bar and Restaurant, Swatragh (028-7940-1206); food all day, open fire, warm welcome.

INFORMATION:

Magherafelt TIC (02879-631510);

www.magherafelt.gov.uk/tourism; www.discovernorthernireland.com.

Carntogher History Trail – see 'Maps' above.

50

VINEGAR HILL LOOP, SPERRIN HILLS, CO TYRONE

TWO SEPARATE BUT RELATED delights awaited Jane and me at the foot of the Barnes Gap – a glorious day of sunshine over the Sperrin Hills, and the sight of Martin McGuigan clambering out of his van with his walking boots on. Inveterate hill walker and mountaineer Martin, fit and springy, is exactly the man you want with you in the Sperrins. This wild range of fells, straddling the waist of County Tyrone, is his native ground; and not only does he know every inch of the hills, he was instrumental in putting together the wonderful Vinegar Hill Looped Walk around the beautiful and lonely glen of Gorticashel.

'Mullaghcarn with the peaked head, down there in the south,' said Martin, pointing out the landscape features from the heights of the narrow Barnes Gap, 'and the central Sperrins all around us here. Then what I'd call the High Sperrins to the north there through the Gap. Of course we'd never have had this view if it wasn't for the Ice Age. The glaciers scraped and shaped all the hills you can see; and then  when they were melting they formed a huge lake, and when *that* overflowed it just burst through a weak spot in the rock and formed the Gap itself.'

A landscape with dynamic origins, and an exceptionally beautiful one. From the old stony road that winds like a scarf around the upper shoulders of the Gorticashel glen we looked down into a silent bowl of fields, some green with good grazing, others hazed under bracken and sedge. Abandoned farmsteads lay dotted across the slopes, each rusted roof of corrugated iron an orange blob among tattered shelter trees – eloquent testimony to the hardships faced by small country farms these days.

'Lazybed strips.' Martin's finger pointed out the corduroy rows on the slopes of the glen. We tried to imagine the work involved in wresting a family's living out of a lazybed. 'I've dug rows like that myself,' Martin observed. 'It's hard enough work. You dig a trench and turn the soil over on to the next ridge, grass to grass, to make a domed top and undercut sides. Spuds and cabbages. The biggest crop I had was half a ton out of ten rows, each maybe 20 yards long. So lazybeds are very effective – but they'd break your back.'

Two ravens passed overhead, planing downwind with a harsh *cronk!* We paused on Vinegar Hill beside one of the tumbledown cottages, its rafters half smothered with fuchsia and Himalayan balsam, its fireplace choked with tendrils of ivy that were feeling their way blindly, like pale tentacles, out into the room among the wrecks of chairs and dresser. Martin fingered the balsam, ruminating. 'These flowers were a big thing in my childhood. The bees would go crazy for them, and we'd see how many we could catch in a jam jar before we got stung!'

Down where the Gorticashel Burn ran under a bridge, a

ferny old mill house stood hard against the bank, with an ancient potato-digging machine on its mossy cobbles. Sparrows went flocking through a cotoneaster bush on a farmhouse wall. At Scotch Town we found the crossroads guarded by a handsome rooster in a tippet of gleaming ginger feathers. Near Garvagh, as we turned for our homeward step, a great roadside shed stood provisioned for the winter with dried sods of turf.

This whole glen speaks eloquently of the life and work of family farms, present and past. Now, with the opening of the Vinegar Hill Loop, cheerful voices will be heard around the abandoned steadings and boots will tread the forgotten green roads of Gorticashel once more.

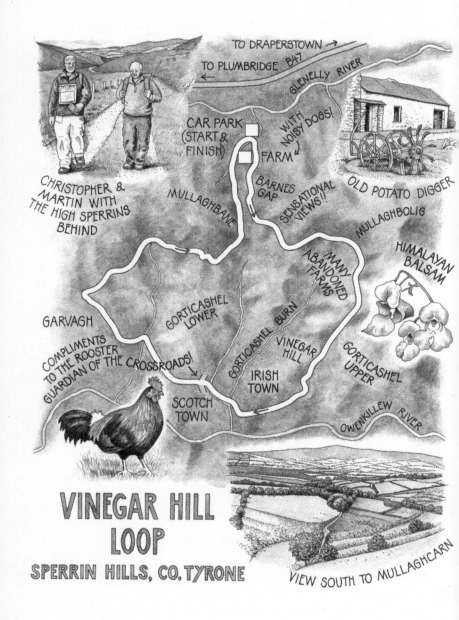

TO DRAPERSTOWN →

← TO PLUMBRIDGE B47

GLENELLY RIVER

CAR PARK (START & FINISH)

WITH NOISY DOGS!

FARM

BARNES GAP

SENSATIONAL VIEWS!!

OLD POTATO DIGGER

MULLAGHBANE

MULLAGHBOLIG

CHRISTOPHER & MARTIN WITH THE HIGH SPERRINS BEHIND

MANY ABANDONED FARMS

HIMALAYAN BALSAM

GORTICASHEL LOWER

GORTICASHEL BURN

VINEGAR HILL

GORTICASHEL UPPER

GARVAGH

COMPLIMENTS TO THE ROOSTER GUARDIAN OF THE CROSSROADS!

IRISH TOWN

OWENKILLEW RIVER

SCOTCH TOWN

VINEGAR HILL LOOP

SPERRIN HILLS, CO. TYRONE

VIEW SOUTH TO MULLAGHCARN

WAY TO GO

MAP: OS of Northern Ireland 1:50,000 Discoverer 13; downloadable map/instructions at www.walkni.com.

TRAVEL: From B74 between Plumbridge and Draperstown, follow brown 'Barnes Gap' tourist signs. Park in car park/toilet/picnic area (OSNI ref. H 551905) at foot of Mullaghbane Road by 'Plumbridge 5' sign.

WALK DIRECTIONS: Walk up the upper Barnes Gap road ('Craignamaddy Circuit/CC, Ulster Way' sign) past farm (barking dogs!). Right along Magherbrack Road for ⅓ mile; left (552896; CC) along dirt road. Follow it round Gorticashel Glen for 2 miles to road near Irish Town (558873). Right for ⅔ mile to crossroads in Scotch Town (548875; 'Gortin' left, 'Plumbridge' right). Straight across here and over next 2 crossroads (544875 and 538880) for 1 mile, to pass turning on left (536883 – tarmac stops here). Ahead for 300 m; right (534885; 'Vinegar Hill Loop') on stony lane. Follow it for 1⅓ miles to road (550892). Forward to Barnes Gap road; left to car park.

LENGTH: 7 miles: allow 3 hours.

GRADE: Easy

CONDITIONS: Minor roads, country lanes.

DON'T MISS:
  views from Barnes Gap – north to High Sperrins, south to Mullaghcarn
  old mill and potato-digger at Scotch Town bridge
  standing stone behind hedge near Garvagh (ref. 538881)

REFRESHMENTS: None en route – take a picnic.

INFORMATION:

Tourist Information Centre, Strule Arts Centre, Omagh; 024-8224-7831; www.discovernorthernireland.com; csomerville@independent.ie.

Walk On The Wild Side 024-8075-8452 or 07714-835-977; www.walkwithmarty.com.

ACKNOWLEDGEMENTS

MY VERY GRATEFUL THANKS are due to Gemma O'Doherty, Travel Editor of the *Irish Independent*, who first suggested I should write a weekly walking piece for the paper. I'm especially grateful to Ciara Scully of Fáilte Ireland for all her help and encouragement. I'd also like to thank Deirdre Byrne and Mark Rowlette of Fáilte Ireland; John Lahiffe and Charlene Boyle of Tourism Ireland; Maeve Curran, Chris Scott, Chris Armstrong and Claire Wright of CAAN; and Claire Keenan of NITB, for all they've done to put me in the way of fabulous walks the length and breadth of Ireland. I'm also grateful to Carey Smith and Hannah Knowles at Ebury Press, and my agent Vivien Green of Sheil Land Associates, for seeing this book through from seed to fruit.

Fáilte Ireland (Republic of Ireland's domestic tourism authority) and Coillte (Forest Service of the Republic of Ireland) have between them helped to open thousands of tracks, trails and Looped Walks for walkers in the Republic, and the same applies to Northern Ireland's CAAN (Countryside Access and Activities Network) and the Forest Service of Northern Ireland.

The hard-worked Rural Recreation Officers are responsible for getting people out walking, developing paths for them to walk on, and initiating, negotiating and maintaining good relations between walkers, farmers, landowners and local authorities – a herculean task they do incredibly well. Many of the paths are built and maintained by members of the RSS, the Rural Social Scheme – an unsung but brilliant initiative to use the practical skills of local people.

Walking companions who have enlivened the way delightfully are John Ahern on the Dingle Way; Seán Ó Súilleabháin, founding father of the Kerry Way long-distance footpath, on the Windy Gap walk on the Iveragh Peninsula; Jimmy Tobin on the Sheep's Head Peninsula on Co Cork; Cal McCarthy of the Ballyhoura Bears on the Canon Sheehan Walk along the borders of Limerick and Cork; Michael Moroney and Jimmy Barry up over Slievenamuck in the Glen of Aherlow; Michael Hickey in the Comeragh Mountains of Co Waterford; Eoin Hogan, Kilkenny county walks officer, on Kilmacoliver Hill; Brian Gilsenan on the Blackstairs Mountains in Co Carlow; Hugh Coogan and Mary O'Connor over Ballycumber Hill in south Wicklow; Pat Liddy bringing the heart of Dublin alive; Michael Murtagh along the River Shannon near Parteen Weir; Olcan Masterson on many magical and musical adventures; Anna Connor and Mary McDonagh on Clogher Bog in the Plains of Mayo; Con Halton and Dominic Halse across Edenmore Bog at Ballinamuck, Co Longford; Oliver Usher on Girley Bog, Co Meath; Aude Laffon and Peádar Quine up in Medbh's Gap under Barnavave, on a very rainy day over Co Louth's Cooley Peninsula; John Ed Sheanon and Peadar Reynolds round Bailieborough and Castle Lake in Co Cava; Inga Bock, Donegal's Rural Recreation Officer, on the Tower Loop at Glencolumbkille; Pat Murphy in the skirts of the Blue Stack Mountains; Ron Murray over Slieve Gullion, Co Armagh; Philip Rollinson and David Thompson around Mount Stewart and Strangford Lough, Co Down; and Martin McGuigan in the Sperrin Hills of Co Tyrone.

Among the many movers and shakers in the world of Irish walking, special help and encouragement have come from Neil Lacey of Gougane Barra Hotel in West Cork; Jim Flynn in the Ballyhoura Mountains; Helen Morrissey of the Glen of Aherlow Fáilte Society, and Ferghal Purcell of Aherlow House Hotel below the Galty Mountains; Hugh and Margaret Coogan of Tinahely, south Wicklow; Treasa Ní Ghearraigh and Uinsíonn Mac Graith of Carrowteige, who lay out walks and keep the Irish language healthy and meaningful in their wild corner of north-west Mayo; Co Leitrim's Jackie Lee, who dispenses walks leaflets and sound advice in his post office/shop at Aghacashel in the shadow of Sliabh an Iarainn; and Gerardine and Eugene Kilet of Laurel Villa, Magherafelt, keepers of the triple flame of poetry, hospitality and the outdoors. Not to mention Frank Fahey, indefatigable surveyor of Looped Walks and eminence not-so-grise of the Irish walking world.

A huge factor in the excellent reception these walks have had from *Irish Independent* readers has been the beauty and accuracy of Claire Littlejohn's wonderful maps. They draw the eye, and hold it, complimenting the words in a way I can't imagine being bettered. So a big thank-you, Claire.

My wife Jane features in many of these walks; she has been my constantly cheerful and encouraging companion, drawing my attention to a million things I'd otherwise have missed.

Lastly, I'm extremely grateful to all the *Irish Independent* readers who have read and followed these walks, and have let me know what was right and wrong with them.

Chistopher Somerville

INDEX

Sheep's Head Peninsula 1, 28, 29, **30**
Sheridan, J.P. 156
Sheriff's Debtors' Prison, Dublin 86, 88
Shielmartin 91
Ship Sound 125
Shirley family (of Lough Fea) 188
Shrough Dolmen 46, 50
Silver Shadows 191
Skean, Lough 152
Skelpoonagh Bay 202
Skunk Hollow 218, 220
Slemish 5, 222, 245
Slí an Easa 32, **34**, 35
Sliabh an Iarainn 4, 191–5, **194**
Sliabh an Iarainn Walking Festival 13
Sliabh na mBan 5, 52
Sliabh Rua 114, 116, 118
Sliabhnamon 57
Slieve Anierin 152
Slieve Bernagh 112
Slieve Bloom Eco Walks Festival 13
Slieve Bloom Mountains 5, 104, **107**
Slieve Bloom Walking Club 12
Slieve Bloom Walking Festival 13
Slieve Croob 228
Slieve Dart 149, 150
Slieve Donard 222
Slieve Foye 177, 180
Slieve Gallion 246
Slieve Gullion 5, 221–5, **224**
Slieve Gullion Courtyard Centre 225
Slieve Gullion Forest Park 225
Slieve League cliffs 203
Slieve Mish 23
Slieve Miskish 28
Slieveanorra 238
Slievebawn 66, 67, **68**, 69, 70
Slievenamon 47, 48, 49, 50
Slievenamuck 2, 5, 46, 47, 48, 50
Sligo (town) 195, 200
Sligo, County 61, 156, 193, 196–7
Sligo Bay 196
Sligo Harbour 196
Sligo mountains 212
Small Bridge pub, Dingle 4, 18
Snout of the Cairn 245, 248
South Armagh 10, 221
South Channel (River Lee) 36
South Gate Bridge, Cork 40
South Main Street, Cork 36, 40
South Mall, Cork 40
South Pole Inn, Anascaul 15, 18
South West Walks Ireland 15
South Wicklow 71, 72
Spailpín Fánach, An 4, 36, 40
Sperrin Hills 3, 5, 8, 222, 238, **252**- see also High
  Sperrins
Spinc cliffs 5, 77, 79
Sruffaunboy 137
St Anne's, Cork 37, 40
St Anne's Church, Bailieborough 181, 185
St Audeon's Gate, Dublin 88

St Columbkille's Church 205
St Columbkille's Well 205
St Finbarr's Oratory 34, 35
St Fin Barre's Cathedral 36, 40
St Ghallagáin church 138
St Helen's 62, 65
St Kevin's Bed 78, 79
St Mary's, Dublin 87
St Michan's Church, Dublin 85–6, 88
St Patrick Street, Cork 40
St Patrick's Cabbage 33
St Stephen's Green, Dublin 88
Stags, The 127
Stags of Broadhaven 6, 142
Strangford Lough 4, 8, 226, 227, **229**, 230
Stratocaster guitars 37, 38
Sturgan Mountain 225
Suffolk 217
Sullivan's Quay, Cork 40
Sunderland flying boats 2, 216, 218
Swatragh 245, 248
sweathouses 151–2
'Sweet Aherlow' 47
Switzerland 7

T.M. Smith Mortgages 181
Taaffe's Castle 180
Táin Bó Cuailnge 176
Táin Way 180
Tara 91
Tara Street, Dublin 88
Temple Bar, Dublin 88
Temple of the Winds 227, **227**
Thompson, David 226–30, **229**
Thoreau, Henry 56
Tierney, Seamus 156
Tinahely 72, **74**, 75
Tinahely Trail Walking Festival 13
Tinahely Walking Club 12
Tipperary (town) 50
Tipperary, County 13, 46, 52, 110
Tir na n'Og 20, 227
Tobar Beannaithe 18
Tobar Eoin 16, 18
Tobin, Bernie 31
Tobin, Jimmy 28–30
Tolkien, J.R.R. 45
Tomduff Hill **68**, 69, 70
Tooreen 31
Tooreen ridge 52
Torc Waterfall 24, **25**, 26
Tourist Information Offices 11
Tower Loop **204**
Town Café, Bailieborough 185
Town Lake, Bailieborough 182, 185
Trá Gheal 125, 128
Trá Mhóir 6, 130, **132**
tradition 3–4
Tráigh na bhFothantaí Dubha 139, 142
Trail Kilkenny 58
Trailhead 75
Tralee 16, 18, 22